CD-ROM
Local Area Networks

Supplements to
COMPUTERS IN LIBRARIES

CD-ROM
Local Area Networks:
A User's Guide

▲

Edited by
Norman Desmarais

Meckler
Westport • London

Library of Congress Cataloging-in-Publication Data

CD-ROM local area networks: a user's guide / edited by Norman
  Desmarais.
        p. cm.--(Supplements to Computers in libraries; 24.)
     Includes bibliographical references and index.
     ISBN 0-88736-700-3 (acid free paper): $
     1. Libraries--Automation. 2. Local area networks (Computer
networks) 3. Microcomputers--Library applications. 4. Optical
disks--Library applications. 5. CD-ROM.   I. Desmarais, Norman.
II. Series.
Z678.93.L63C38   1991
020'.285 ' 468--dc20   90-28338
                                                             CIP

British Library Cataloguing in Publication Data

CD-ROM local area networks: A user's guide.
  I. Desmarais, Norman
  025.04

  ISBN 0-88736-700-3

Meckler Publishing, the publishing division of Meckler Corporation,
  11 Ferry Lane West, Westport, CT 06880.
Meckler Ltd., 247-249 Vauxhall Bridge Road,
  London SW1V 1HQ, U.K.

Printed on acid free paper.
Printed and bound in the United States of America.

Contents

Introduction

When *The Librarian's CD-ROM Handbook* first appeared, the idea of mounting CD-ROM products on a local area network still had not come to maturity. A few companies had products in the testing stage. Some of these products did not get to market; others appeared for a short time, only to be withdrawn and redesigned.

Most users could not afford to subscribe to many titles. Prices for both titles and drives remained high. Few had multiple workstations with CD-ROM drives attached. Many had to operate their stations in dedicated mode to support heavy use of a single title. Operating costs to buy additional computers and CD-ROM drives and pay for new title subscriptions presented obstacles to market expansion.

CD-ROM publishers feared the threat of losing a still-tiny market. They worried about the prospect of selling a single disc and having every PC owner access it. Information providers wrestled--and continue to do so--with pricing structures, copyright issues, and licensing agreements.

Librarians have witnessed many changes in the two years that have elapsed since then. We now have several hardware and software options to choose from. We anticipate others emerging in the near future.

The installation and setup of CD-ROM drives and software can sometimes create confusion for those not versed in the technicalities of the PC environment. Setting up a local area network for CD-ROM compounds this situation. Not only do the original problems remain; but now we have added the complexities of setting up and operating a local area network with all that implies: the complexities of hardware and software selection, setup, integration, and operation; network administration; file management and security; and more.

This book attempts to address these issues and to explain the various options to consider or the questions to ask when considering setting up a local area network for CD-ROM applications. We explore local area networks in general and the implications for CD-ROM. We look at the variety of software and hardware options currently available. We discuss the implications for the system manager or network administrator. We also consider alternatives to networking and future possibilities as well as copyright and licensing issues.

The contributors have all successfully installed local area networks. These networks all differ in their configurations; and the contributors--vendor representatives as well as librarians from academic and public libraries--bring a variety of perspectives to our discussion of this topic.

Norman Desmarais

1
CD-ROM and LANs
Mark Leggott

Without a doubt, two of the most talked-about microcomputer technologies of today include networks and CD-ROM. Both have been around for a number of years; and both have reached a high level of maturity. This book, therefore, is very timely. One or two years ago, if you wanted to network CD-ROM products, you had very limited options for how to accomplish that task. Today, a number of solutions exist for the full range of systems (as other chapters in this book indicate), from microcomputers to mainframes; and these solutions are now easier to implement.

This chapter will give a brief overview of networks and the advantages of implementing them, particularly where CD-ROMs play an important role. The literature has many excellent and in-depth books and articles on networks, as the bibliography at the end of the book indicates.

Introduction

The term "network" gets wide use in the computer industry. This has led to some confusion as to exactly what constitutes a network. The industry often misuses the term in order to help sell products which have nothing to do with networks; and this contributes to the confusion. In general, we may define a network as *two or more computers connected together by some form of communication medium*. This connection may consist of the traditional wire or something more advanced like infrared beams of light or radio waves. The types of computers that get connected together may also vary. For example, we can link IBM PCs, MACs, or a combination of both.

Starting with this general definition, one can derive many permutations and combinations ranging from the often mentioned *Nike* or *Sneaker Net* (here, the connection between computers consists of

1

someone with a good pair of running shoes), to a state-of-the-art, fibre optic network spanning a continent. I will concern myself primarily with *Local Area Networks* (LAN) which we can further qualify as computers in a distinct "local area", such as an office, a floor, or an entire building. Once this more-or-less permanent connection involves broader links, such as using telecommunications wire to link to more distant components, we usually refer to the network as a *Metropolitan Area Network* (MAN) or a *Wide Area Network* (WAN), depending on the extent of the geographic area covered. As with all definitions, this distinction may blur, but LANs are generally well defined entities with discrete components.

The initial flurry of activity which follows the introduction of a new technology and gives rise to a plethora of products is settling as far as LAN hardware is concerned. Eighty to ninety percent of LAN systems use Ethernet, ARCnet, or Token Ring hardware (discussed in more detail in chapters 2 and 3). Much of the activity in this area concentrates on making LAN products better, faster, and more compatible. For example, many of the newer interface cards will let you use either twisted pair, coaxial, or fibre optic wiring for the same price as one which used to limit you to one of these connections. Also, the wide acceptance of NetBIOS as a LAN system standard (akin to having a Hayes compatible modem or an IBM compatible computer) has helped to make setting up a network a little less of a headache. NetBIOS consists of a set of system-level commands which defines how networked computers talk to each other; so components which support it should get along just fine.

In addition, LANs no longer constitute only a physical link between computers; they are themselves redefining computing. For example, new terms like *groupware* and *workgroup computing* have their basis in closely integrated systems of computers and people. The question no longer remains "How can I get these computers to talk to each other?" but "How can I get these computers/people to work together more efficiently and productively?" While we may be tempted to say that we are simply harkening back to the days of mainframes and dumb terminals, networking consists of much more today. The power of personal computing together with the advantages of strong intercommunication results in much more than the sum of its parts.

Parts of a LAN

The major parts of a LAN comprise the computers (both workstations and servers), network interface cards (NICs), cabling, and software.

The traditional LAN system connects personal computers, either IBM compatible, Macintoshes, or both. A network may include a wide variety of PCs, ranging from IBM XTs to the latest 486 machines. Cheap computers with little or no hard disk storage can offer much more utility when attached to a powerful server on a network. As a result, computer workstations have tended to consist of low-end PCs with monochrome monitors. However, as the price of computers continues to come down (you can buy an XT for as little as $500), many workstations make use of color and faster central processing units (CPUs), such as those using an 80286 or more powerful microprocessor. Since many newer software packages make good use of color (particularly CD-ROM applications), color monitors are recommended. Some public access areas have also opted for diskless workstations. These workstations increase system security by preventing users from rebooting with their own floppy disks.

While networks may incorporate dumb terminals (those with no memory storage and processing capabilities), many CD-ROM applications require a hard disk for creating and storing temporary files and for local processing.

One limiting factor with many PC networks comes in the amount of RAM, or system memory, available for application software and the network. When a workstation signs on to a network, it must use part of its system memory for the network operating system. With applications such as CD-ROM software, which are traditionally very RAM-hungry, this can present a severe problem. There are a number of ways to reduce memory problems, including: making sure that workstations have a minimum of 640K of memory (and preferably 1MB), using "extended" memory cards (such as High-Card Plus) and using memory management software in combination with 386SX or 386 computers. Chapter 2 will discuss this issue in more detail.

Network Servers

Network servers generally tend to consist of high-end PCs to maximize the speed of activity on the network. Also, newer network software (such as Netware 386) aims to take full advantage of the

32-bit processing power of 386 and 486 CPUs, resulting in significant performance advantages. In a network situation other factors, such as a fast hard drive or extra memory for caching, can also increase the performance of a network server.

Network Interface Card

The network interface card (NIC) provides the physical and logical link from the workstations to other computers on the network. Generally installed in a spare slot in the computer, newer external NICs are useful for laptop computers or for those that have few available slots. The NIC communicates with the computer in which it resides and packages any network requests in a format suitable for transport across the network. NICs come in many shapes and sizes. Some proprietary NICs are designed for use with specific network software. For example, LANtastic manages to limit the amount of system memory required by supporting many LAN functions in ROM chips on the NIC. Other cards may provide a range of choices for LAN cabling or offer greater flexibility in reducing conflicts with other cards in the PC. The NIC also determines the speed of transmitting information packets on the network to match the installed cabling.

Cables

LAN cabling can also present some confusion in the number of types available. Today, we have three basic cabling systems in use: twisted-pair (phone cable), coaxial (the familiar cable-TV wire), and fibre optic. The cables are listed here in order of low to high price and low to high speed. The different types of cable also vary in the distance between workstations and servers/other workstations they can handle. The type of cable used will depend on an institution's individual characteristics and needs. For example, an increasing number of large university networks incorporate fibre optic cable, as it allows for maximum speed; and it can extend over longer distances. Large installations such as this may also make use of various devices such as *repeaters, routers,* and *bridges* to augment or modify signals over long distances. Newer technologies use light or radio waves to send information between computers.

LAN Software

LAN software also comes in many shapes and sizes and often presents the most difficult choice in setting up a LAN. The most common networking system is Novell which uses a proprietary protocol called IPX and which appears in numerous incarnations. While it has a reputation for being difficult to set up, the newer 386 version is much easier to work with. The other major protocol is NetBIOS, which an increasing number of software vendors in the IBM PC market, including Novell, either support or emulate. Other major protocols include MS-NET, Appleshare (for MACs), TOPS (for IBMs and MACs), and TCP/IP (Transmission Control Protocol/Internet Protocol). The latter's importance comes particularly in network configurations which aim to link different computer systems (PCs, minis, and mainframes). Some examples of LAN systems include LANtastic, Net/30, and GV LAN OS (low-end); Novell 286 and IBM PC LAN (mid-range); and Novell 386 and 3COM 3+ Open (high-end).

The price of LAN systems obviously spans a wide range. The price per node for both hardware and software will range from $250 for a peer-to-peer system to $2000 for a high-end, client-server application (we define these terms below). Also, hardware and software support/maintenance could add an additional $5000 or more over a 5-year period. Depending on the system configuration, you may also require a LAN administrator.

Types of LANs

There are a number of ways to accomplish the interconnections which characterize a LAN; and the sophistication of these links vary widely.

Originally, a LAN principally aimed at printer sharing--usually an expensive laser printer. Smaller offices can accomplish this with mechanical or electronic *printer switches.* These devices carry varying degrees of sophistication (e.g. sophisticated printer buffering/spooling); but, essentially, all provide simple links for multiple computers to one or more printers. Needless to say, this falls short of a functional LAN and is not much use to those of us who want to share CD-ROM products.

Zero Slot LANs

Zero slot LANs (ZSLANs) or serial LANs, resemble full blown LANs, except they use a spare serial port or, less often, a parallel port to connect machines. Therefore, they do not need a special card installed in each computer (hence the designation zero slot LAN). Again, the functionality of ZSLANs vary; but they do allow access to files on other people's machines; and you can transfer files without disturbing the user of the other machine. Some will also let you share printers, CD-ROM drives, and other peripherals. Keep in mind that most ZSLANs will not let you run the special LAN version of application programs, as they usually omit all the features needed to support simultaneous access to an application (i.e. editing or file maintenance).

Also, ZSLANs are very slow when compared to full-blown LANs, as the speed of the port limits them. Working with a slow device such as a CD-ROM drive would make this even more noticeable. Thus, a ZSLAN would operate at a maximum of 115,200 bps (bits per second), while traditional LANs transfer information at speeds ranging from 2 to 16 Mbps (megabits per second).

The more traditional LANs, and the ones we are most concerned with here, come in two basic flavors--Peer-to-Peer (PPLAN), and Client-Server (CSLAN).

Peer-to-Peer LANs

PPLANs generally consist of low-end systems designed for occasional use of shared resources or for smaller installations (1-10 nodes). They are characterized by the fact that anyone on the network can both provide and use network resources (e.g. files, CD-ROM drives), and still use their computer for the normal functions--hence the name. LANtastic (see chapter 2) is a popular PPLAN which allows sharing of CD-ROM drives. However, the access speed drops precipitously as soon as two or more individuals use the drive at the same time. Also, unless you use high-end hardware (386 or 486 CPUs), you will find the speed of your word processor or spreadsheet slows dramatically as other computers access yours via the LAN. Needless to say, if you had such high-end hardware, you could probably afford a high-end LAN!

Significant economic gains offset the slower retrieval speed. PPLANs are inexpensive (a few hundred dollars per node); so we can recommend them in situations where money comprises a key consideration. Also, some PPLANs allow you to set up one computer as a *dedicated* server, so that CPU power is devoted solely to requests from the network. Other PPLANs which allow sharing CD-ROM drives include GV LAN OS (significantly faster than LANtastic) and Net/30. Both have costs ranging from $200 to $300 per node, including cards, cable, and software. Where CD-ROM resources form an important component of the network system (i.e. heavily used), a peer-to-peer LAN may not offer the best alternative. CD-ROM drives are slow compared to other devices, such as hard drives. Anything which accentuates this characteristic may lead to unacceptable performance in some situations.

Client-Server LANs

Where sharing of CD-ROMs presents an important factor, a *Client-Server* LAN may be more appropriate. CSLANs are designed for occasional to heavy use of shared resources or for medium to large installations (6 to 100+ nodes). In this situation, one or more computers are identified as servers--they provide shared resources for other computers on the network. Generally these computers consist of *dedicated* servers that do not get used for any other purpose. Since the server's CPU is dedicated to handling requests from the network, it operates faster and much more efficiently. This increased speed/efficiency is matched by an increased price, both in terms of the dedicated hardware and, generally, higher-cost software. However, most librarians who need to provide network access to CD-ROMs will probably find themselves looking at a CSLAN.

It is interesting to note that one often hears that CSLANs are more difficult to administer, while PPLANs are easier and less cumbersome. This probably relates to the fact that PPLANs tend to be much smaller than CSLANs and, therefore, have fewer users to worry about. However, I think we can safely say that any network has significant administrative overhead, regardless of the type. In a situation where you have different users accessing files on remote computers, the usual problems associated with single-user computers are accentuated. In fact, a large PPLAN may be more difficult to administer than a similarly sized CSLAN, since each user can share/use any available resources. As a result, it is more difficult to keep track of what is going on.

In terms of sharing CD-ROMs, CSLANs have some distinct advantages over PPLANs. As previously mentioned, they make full use of dedicated equipment, giving a faster response time. This is very important for CD-ROM applications. CD-ROM products are generally critical resources (i.e. heavily used and expensive), so effective use of these resources is important. Also, the number of times that a shared CD-ROM drive is accessed is high (in comparison to word processors, etc.), increasing the amount of network traffic and, consequently, the load on the computer providing access to the CD-ROMs. Since CD-ROM has finally reached critical mass, the use of CD-ROM products will increase within the next twelve months; and the demand to have access to them will also increase.

Why Put a CD-ROM on a LAN?

Reasons for implementing LANs are numerous; but certainly one of the most persuasive and oft-cited reasons involves the economic benefits received from allowing multiple users to share expensive components (printers, high-capacity hard drives, CD-ROM drives/ products). Other general reasons include:

File/Application sharing: LANs make it easy to share files (even across different platforms, such as DOS to MAC) or send them to others on the system. This ability forms the basis of the network's electronic mail facilities.

Increased data integrity: All users of a central database can have confidence that they all have access to the same information. It is easier to control the input of new data on a network, since only certain individuals can receive the authority to update files. Different LAN systems afford more or less protections in this area; so be careful that you get what you expect.

Increased security: New LAN systems use increasingly sophisticated methods to ensure control of access to shared resources. This can present an important consideration in a library/information center setting, where the computer will remain unattended most of the time.

Increased "productivity": The number of new "groupware" and related products promising to promote the productivity of work groups continues to increase. While not yet in wide use, this promises to become one of the more active areas of growth within the LAN market.

While one generally does not install a LAN simply to share CD-ROMs, CD-ROM products are becoming increasingly important as shared network resources for a number of important reasons. We already mentioned the first, the economics of sharing. The price of CD-ROM hardware continues to fall; so, in many respects, this does not present a critical consideration. What is critical is the price of CD-ROM products. While most vendors currently levy additional charges for a LAN license, the amount varies. As more and more institutions network CD-ROM products, more economically attractive networking policies will become commonplace.

Putting CD-ROMs on larger networks also allows older equipment, such as dumb terminals tied to the mainframe, to access this information. For example, Gandalf makes a system called Starport which ties dumb terminals into dedicated PC boards which can then link into a Meridian CD Net for access to CD-ROM drives. This system is being used to provide access to traditional CD-ROM indexes from regional offices and also to set up cataloguing facilities (using LaserGuide) in remote libraries communicating with a mini-computer via phone lines.

Remote Access

This also highlights the feasibility of remote access to the wealth of information on CD-ROM, including public domain software collections and traditional reference tools. Regional offices or distance learners at a large university can receive the same access accorded to those at the main office or campus. They simply dial in to the dedicated CD-ROM server via standard phone lines, using standard communications software. With some commercial applications this raises a number of tricky licensing questions which chapter 7 will discuss in more detail.

This networking capability accommodates linking with WORM (write once, read many) technology from companies like Yamaha and Fuji (which allows producing "one-off" copies of industry-standard

CD-ROM discs in-house) to create extensive information archives on low-cost CD-ROM hardware.

For example, some companies place their central records on the corporate network using this technology. They can also replicate the data at any time (e.g. for regional offices) in a standard CD facility since it already conforms to the High Sierra or ISO 9660 format. Some institutions are also investigating the potential of archiving their massive 9-track tape libraries onto CD-ROM and then making them available on networked CD-ROM towers or jukebox systems. They can now store the data in an inexpensive CD rack instead of in a massive climate-controlled tape-mausoleum with around-the-clock technicians and cleaning equipment!

Finally, CD-ROMs can add significantly to the new concept of workgroup computing which is evolving along with networking technology. Further, they will enhance the power of people working together with computers.

2
CD-ROM Network Software
Oliver Pesch

On the surface, adding CD-ROM networking to a Local Area Network may seem like a simple enough task--just locate the appropriate networking hardware and software and away you go. Unfortunately, it isn't quite as easy as that--as many who have gone through the exercise can attest.

With several CD-ROM networking solutions on the market, potential buyers must consider a number of questions before purchasing a CD-ROM network: What CD-ROM networking software works with what network operating system? Will the networking software be compatible with the programs you want to run? Will the workstations have enough RAM available to run the CD-ROM applications? Does the software make the CD-ROM network access quick enough to produce acceptable response time for the users?

This chapter aims to provide the reader with enough insight into the workings of CD-ROM network software to be able to make an intelligent analysis of the options available. Later in the chapter, we present some brief descriptions of the features of some of the CD-ROM network solutions on the market. Please keep in mind that this information was compiled in August of 1990; and the data contained therein may have changed. Please call the various vendors and ask the pertinent questions.

Definition of Terms

Before we get into the details of how the networking of CD-ROM works, we need to define a few terms:

CD-ROM Application: a product that usually consists of search and retrieval software that accesses a database contained on a CD-ROM disc.

11

CD-ROM Networking: software that allows workstations on a local area network to access CD-ROM players on another computer (the CD-ROM server) on the same network.

Device Driver: a program that allows the operating system to recognize a non-standard device--one which the operating system itself does not address directly. A CD-ROM player requires access through a device driver.

Expanded Memory: The MS-DOS operating system only allows the operating system and application programs to use 640K of RAM (random access memory). To get around this barrier, Lotus, Intel, and Microsoft agreed upon a standard method of expanding memory beyond the DOS limit. This standard--known as "expanded," LIM (for Lotus, Intel, Microsoft), or EMS memory--allows applications to allocate memory beyond the DOS limit by breaking this memory into "pages" that can be "mapped" into regular DOS memory for use. One adds expanded memory on an 8088 computer through a separate memory card. Computers with the 80286 or 80386 microprocessors have the added capability of allowing their "extended" memory to emulate expanded memory by using special device drivers or memory managers.

Extended Memory: The 8088 processors used in IBM PCs and compatibles only have the capability to address directly 1 MB of RAM. The 80286 processor, built with the ability to address 16MB of RAM, greatly increased this limit. We refer to the memory above the first MB in an 80286 and 80386 computer as "extended" memory. Unfortunately, the 640K limit still exists for most MS-DOS programs. As only a very few programs have the capability of using extended memory, a common option uses a memory manager or device driver to allow the extended memory to emulate "expanded memory."

High Sierra Standard: a standard established by CD-ROM producers for the volume and file format for CD-ROM. This has since evolved into the ISO 9660 standard.

Local Area Network (LAN): two or more interconnected computers, usually in the same facility, that share resources. Typically, the computers are connected by coaxial, twisted pair, or similar cable capable of transferring data at a very high speed--at least 2 Mbps (megabits per second).

Microsoft MS-DOS CD-ROM Extensions: a program that allows access to CD-ROM discs created to the High Sierra or ISO 9660 standards to resemble a large DOS disk. This allows producers of CD-ROM products to make applications that are compatible with virtually all makes of CD-ROM drives. (Synonymous terms, often used interchangeably, include *Extensions* or *Microsoft Extensions*.)

Redirector: network software which runs in the workstation and intercepts any disk activity (reads, writes, etc.) that are intended for a network drive and "redirects" these to the appropriate server. Redirectors also "redirect" printed output to the printer server in the same manner.

Server: a computer on the network which controls resources that other workstations on the network share. A file server shares its hard disk space; a printer server shares its printers; and a CD-ROM server shares its CD-ROM players.

Standard DOS Routines: This term describes the basic DOS services (e.g. opening and reading files) an application developer uses to access files on a DOS hard disk. For CD-ROM discs, Microsoft CD-ROM Extensions intercepts calls to these routines, then obtains the information from the CD-ROM.

Third Party Software: software purchased from someone other than the maker of the local area network but which is designed to work with that network. Both Online Computer Products and Meridian Data offer third party software that allow CD-ROM networking on Novell and other networks.

Workstation: a computer on a local area network which does local processing. Frequently, a workstation consists of an IBM PC, XT, AT, PS/2 or compatible.

How CD-ROM Applications Access the CD-ROM

Microsoft Extensions compatibility is the one common denominator for all networkable CD-ROM products. Before we become involved in the details of CD-ROM network software, let's step back for a moment and look at non-networked CD-ROM applications. Understanding how CD-ROM applications obtain data from the CD-ROM drive will help in understanding the issues with the various techniques used in networking CD-ROMs.

The following diagram illustrates what happens when Microsoft Extensions accesses data from a CD-ROM disc. For the purpose of the illustrations in this chapter, we will assume that the CD-ROM has been assigned to drive **L:**. (Microsoft Extensions assigns the actual drive letter for a CD-ROM, so this may vary from computer to computer).

Figure 1.

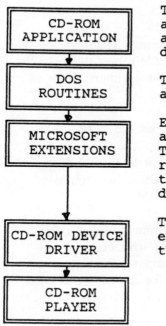

The CD-ROM application issues a READ for data on drive L: (the CD-ROM).

The READ is processed as a normal DOS read.

EXTENSIONS intercepts all reads for drive L: The read request is reformatted and sent to the CD-ROM device driver.

The device driver extracts the data from the CD-ROM player.

In Figure 1, we see how a read request was issued to DOS, intercepted by Microsoft Extensions, and passed on to the CD-ROM device driver. The data is read from the CD-ROM and passed back up the chain.

Products that use the model depicted in Figure 1 offer the most flexibility in terms of CD-ROM networking as they will operate on virtually any CD-ROM network. The CD-ROM application uses only standard DOS routines to read the information. Therefore, it runs exactly as if it were accessing a database on a hard disk.

Unfortunately, not all products follow this simple model. In defining the High Sierra format, the CD-ROM producers addressed some of the unique attributes of databases on CD-ROM. A CD-ROM producer may want control over the date when a database becomes effective or when that database expires. To accommodate these requirements and others, the High Sierra Standard allows, including on the CD-ROM, information such as the origination date, effective date, expiry date, publisher, and more. DOS cannot access this additional information. Therefore, Microsoft provided a way for CD-ROM applications to bypass the standard DOS routines and communicate directly with Microsoft Extensions to find out this information. Several of the more sophisticated CD-ROM applications use this direct interface with Microsoft Extensions.

Still other CD-ROM applications communicate directly with the CD-ROM device driver, bypassing both DOS routines and Microsoft Extensions. A CD-ROM application can test the status of the CD-ROM player through the device driver to ensure that the disc has not been removed. The application can also lock the CD-ROM player door or eject the CD-ROM disc from the player. Some of the older CD-ROM applications (created prior to the existence of Microsoft Extensions) will read data from the CD-ROM directly through the device driver and not use Microsoft Extensions at all.

The following diagram illustrates the two variations on Figure 1.

Figure 2.

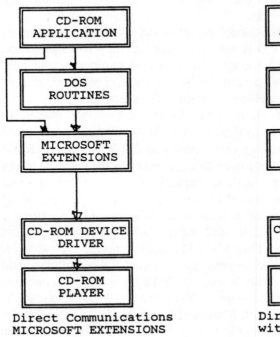
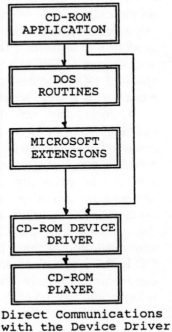

Direct Communications   Direct Communications
MICROSOFT EXTENSIONS   with the Device Driver

The left side of Figure 2 has an additional line which depicts the CD-ROM application communicating directly with Microsoft Extensions as well as through the standard DOS routines. The diagram on the right depicts an application that communicates directly with the device driver. As mentioned earlier, some CD-ROM applications bypass Microsoft Extensions completely and communicate directly with the device driver to read data from the CD-ROM. Other applications use this facility to check the status of the CD-ROM to determine if a disc has been removed or changed.

The techniques of communicating directly with Microsoft Extensions and the device driver are completely valid. Unfortunately these techniques, while helpful for the CD-ROM application developer, create a challenge to the network software developer.

Two Methods for Accessing CD-ROM Data Across a Network

The simplest way to share CD-ROM data across a network allows the network file server to share the CD-ROM disc as if it were just another network drive. Artisoft uses this approach with their LANtastic Network Operating System. The LANtastic network redirector, "redirects" all DOS disk access requests to the server--including requests for CD-ROM data. The CD-ROM appears to the workstation as just another network drive.

Figure 3 depicts how a network system with the CD-ROM drive redirected in the same manner as a network hard disk would process a request for CD-ROM data. Again, we use drive L: to represent the CD-ROM drive.

Figure 3.

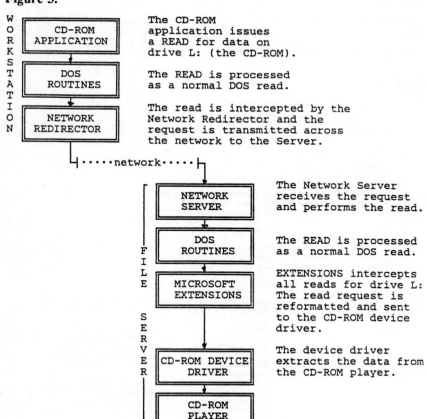

W
O
R
K
S
T
A
T
I
O
N

| CD-ROM APPLICATION | The CD-ROM application issues a READ for data on drive L: (the CD-ROM). |

| DOS ROUTINES | The READ is processed as a normal DOS read. |

| NETWORK REDIRECTOR | The read is intercepted by the Network Redirector and the request is transmitted across the network to the Server. |

·····network·····

F
I
L
E

S
E
R
V
E
R

| NETWORK SERVER | The Network Server receives the request and performs the read. |

| DOS ROUTINES | The READ is processed as a normal DOS read. |

| MICROSOFT EXTENSIONS | EXTENSIONS intercepts all reads for drive L: The read request is reformatted and sent to the CD-ROM device driver. |

| CD-ROM DEVICE DRIVER | The device driver extracts the data from the CD-ROM player. |

| CD-ROM PLAYER |

While this approach is very effective for some products (those that follow the model depicted in Figure 1), it does create difficulties for products that use direct calls to Microsoft Extensions or the CD-ROM device driver (Figure 2). Because neither Microsoft Extensions nor the device driver operate in the workstation (they run in the server), these direct calls fail and the CD-ROM application will not work.

Third party software developers such as Online Computer Products (OPTI-NET) and Meridian Data Inc. (CD-NET) take another approach to networking CD-ROM data. They do not rely on network redirectors to access the CD-ROM data on the server. Instead, they replace the CD-ROM device driver with a special device driver that communicates the requests for CD-ROM data to the CD-ROM server. Because this device driver operates--at least on the surface--in exactly the same manner as a regular CD-ROM device driver, Microsoft Extensions and the CD-ROM application remain unaware of any CD-ROM access across the network. The following diagram shows how this system would process a read operation.

Figure 4.

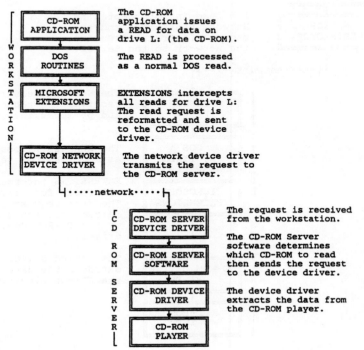

This technique has the advantage that an application can successfully make direct calls to Microsoft Extensions or to the CD-ROM device driver. This means that virtually any CD-ROM application that runs on a stand-alone CD-ROM workstation can also operate on this type of network.

Unfortunately, this approach has drawbacks. In most cases, the CD-ROM server must remain separate from the network file server, resulting in the need to purchase an extra computer.[1] Also, having Microsoft Extensions and the device driver loaded in the workstation may limit the amount of RAM free for running the CD-ROM application--resulting in the inability to run some products.[2]

Complete CD-ROM Network Solutions

A number of companies offer what we will call a complete solution to CD-ROM networking. Companies in this category would include Online Computer Products Corporation (OPTI-NET), Meridian Data, Inc. (CD-NET), EBSCO Electronic Information (EBSCO's CD-ROM Network), and SilverPlatter (MultiPlatter). These solutions go beyond simply providing shared access to CD-ROM. They offer additional features such as:

Menu Program. This provides users with a simple single interface to access all products on the network. The menu program usually has a feature which prevents the user from getting access to the DOS prompt.

Usage Tracking. Normally an extension to the menu program, usage tracking basically logs the number of times someone accesses the various applications and records the duration. Statistical reporting programs allow tracking system use over various time periods by date, product, or workstation. Knowing which products get extensive use and which do not can provide valuable information at budget time. Without usage tracking on a large CD-ROM network, one would find it very difficult to determine, for example, which products get such infrequent use that they do not merit renewal.

Limit Number of Users by Product. This feature has two objectives. By setting a limit for the number of simultaneous users on a product, the institution has a way of enforcing limits imposed by license agreements. One can mount more than one copy of a heavily used database on a network and automatically balance its use across the network with this feature.

Session Time Limit. On a busy network, users can have their time in a particular database restricted. If they exceed the time on the workstation, a warning message appears regularly until they log off.

Common Exit Keys. CD-ROM applications running on networks have one major problem: they do not have a common method for exiting. When users want to change to another database, they must know the exit key sequence for the current product before they can return to the menu. A common exit key feature on a CD-ROM network eliminates this problem by allowing use of a single key sequence to exit any product on the network.

Inactivity Time-Out. With this feature, the workstations will automatically return to the product menu after a user-defined number of minutes of inactivity.

Network Status Monitoring. The CD-ROM server often allows monitoring of the activity on the CD-ROM network, providing information such as: the product loaded on a workstation; how long a workstation has been using a product; or how many users are currently searching a given product.

User-Defined Questionnaires. Librarians who want to survey the users on the various aspects of the system or to gather statistical information on user demographics can establish questionnaires which automatically get activated on entry into the system or into a particular product. The program logs results of the question-naires to a disk file, allowing the library staff to analyze and manipulate the data.

Dial-in Access to CD-ROM Databases. With this feature, users can access and search CD-ROM databases remotely. In general, any user with an IBM PC, MAC, or terminal with communications software and a modem can connect to the CD-ROM network and search the databases.

This requires special equipment on the local area network to provide the dial-in ports. This equipment can take the form of a dedicated computer on the network equipped with a modem and phone line and running a communications program such as PC ANYWHERE or Carbon Copy. Typically, one such computer will handle a single remote user at a time. Therefore, to support four simultaneous remote users would require four such computers.

For a more sophisticated solution, one could use an 80386 computer (with lots of RAM) and configure it to handle several simultaneous users. This would also require multi-tasking software (such as Windows or DesqView) as well as the communications software. The 80386 will require a modem and phone line for each concurrent user.

Simplified Installation of CD-ROM Applications. The installation of CD-ROM application software can present a tedious task on large networks because it usually involves individual installation of many CD-ROM applications on each workstation--typically on a local hard drive. Some network solutions, such as EBSCO's CD-ROM Network, come with utilities which automatically distribute software changes to the workstations on the network.

Customer Service. Customer service is a very important consideration. While solutions that take most of the guess work out of loading and running CD-ROM products on a network exist, there always seems to be a myriad of little things to know and remember. Having a good customer support staff to call on will save countless hours of trial and error.

Local Area Network Hardware and Software

This seems the appropriate time in our discussion of CD-ROM networking software to consider the available choices of LAN hardware solutions. In our earlier definition of a local area network, we mentioned that a LAN consists of two or more interconnected computers that share resources. To "interconnect" these computers requires local area network hardware. The local area network software accomplishes "sharing of resources."

To provide a basic understanding of LAN hardware and software, we will look at three things:

- Network topology--the physical way the network hardware is connected.
- Local area network hardware--the options for physically moving the data from one network interface card to another.
- Local area network software--the "smarts" of a local area network that allow the actual sharing of resources.

Network Topologies

The local area network hardware generally consists of network interface cards (installed in each workstation on the network) and the cable used to connect the network interface cards together. This network hardware provides the physical method of transferring data from one computer to the next. The manner of connecting the cable from one computer to the next is often referred to as the network topology. We now describe the three most common topologies.

BUS Topology. In the BUS topology, the network cable travels from one computer to the next in a daisy chain fashion. A special device called a terminator attaches to the "open" cable at either end of the bus. The terminator prevents signals from reflecting back across the network and causing miscommunications among the computers on the network.

RING Topology. The RING topology pretty much resembles the BUS topology in that it connects the computers in a daisy-chain fashion. The difference lies in a cable that extends from the last computer on the network back to the first to close the "ring."

Figure 5. *BUS Topology*

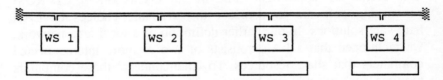

Figure 6. *RING Topology*

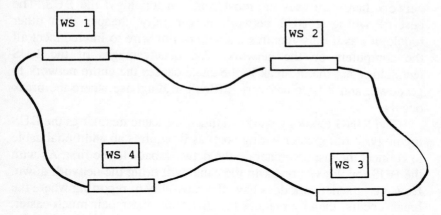

STAR Topology. In the STAR topology all the computers get connected to a central point, either a server or a special network device called a controller or a HUB.

Figure 7. *STAR Topology*

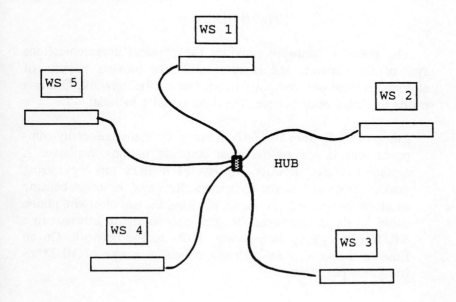

Each of the topologies has advantages and disadvantages. Ethernet network hardware uses the most common topology: the BUS. The cost of wiring a BUS network is generally cheaper than other topologies as it only requires a single run of wire to interconnect all the computers on the network. The disadvantages of the BUS technology are that a break in the cable causes the entire network to go down; and it becomes very difficult to diagnose where the break occurs.

The RING topology works in much the same manner as the BUS topology. It has greater wiring costs as it requires an additional cable to connect the last computer on the network back to the first. As with the BUS topology, a break in the cable will bring the network down. However, the network does have the capability of reporting where the break occurs, thereby making the diagnosis and repair much easier.

The STAR topology is probably the most robust of the three. In most cases a break in the cable will only affect the one computer and the network will continue to run. On most STAR topology networks, the network administrator can add or remove workstations without taking down the entire network. The disadvantage of the STAR topology usually comes in the cost, as it requires a separate run of cable from the central HUB to each workstation.

Network Hardware

The network hardware provides the physical communications layer of the network and is responsible for moving packets of information from one computer to another on the network. One has several available options here. The most popular include:

Ethernet (IEEE standard 802.3). Found on many university campuses, this is one of the most common options available. A typical Ethernet network consists of a BUS topology using coaxial cable to link the computers. Recently, Ethernet became available for twisted pair cable, allowing the use of 4-wire phone cable for the connections. One can also configure Ethernet in a STAR topology by introducing HUBs to the network. On an Ethernet network, data typically travels at a rate of 10 Mbps (megabits per second).

IBM Token Ring (IEEE standard 802.5). This network hardware uses special twisted pair cable to connect the computers on a TOKEN RING topology. The data transfer rate of TOKEN RING is 16 Mbps.

ARCnet. Originally developed by Datapoint Corporation, ARCnet uses coaxial cable in a STAR topology to interconnect computers. The data transfer rate of ARCnet is typically 2.5 Mbps. However, the new ARCnet Plus offers a speeded up version that has a transfer rate of 20 Mbps.

Network Software

The network software provides the intelligence to the local area network. The network software has responsibility for such things as redirecting printed output to a print server or disk activity to a file server. Most network software packages will operate on the network hardware listed above. Many of the network software packages do not provide the built-in capacity for sharing CD-ROM data. To add this capability, one must purchase additional third party software such as OPTI-NET, CD-NET, or CD-CONNECTION. (Frequently, this also requires purchase of a separate CD-ROM server.)

The following list covers the network software packages you will most likely encounter and what hardware they are compatible with.

Novell Advanced Netware. Advanced Netware offers a very popular LAN software package. Netware can run on virtually any network hardware including Ethernet, IBM Token Ring, and ARCnet. Novell requires a dedicated file server. The Novell file server software does NOT include the capability to share CD-ROM data.

3COM. 3COM is another popular network software package that runs on Ethernet hardware. As with Novell, the 3COM server program does NOT include the ability to share CD-ROM data.

LANtastic. LANtastic comprises a low cost network solution that runs on either twisted pair cable using LANtastic's proprietary network hardware or on standard Ethernet hardware. The LANtastic server program will also allow sharing CD-ROMs on the server. LANtastic will accommodate CD-ROM applications which use standard DOS routines exclusively to communicate with the CD-ROM (see Figure 1). Those applications which interface directly with Microsoft Extensions or the CD-ROM device driver will not run.

The CD-ROM network solutions under consideration may sway the choice of network hardware, software, and topology. Predetermined policies of an organization may also mandate selecting one option rather than another. As we focus on the software to network CD-ROMs, further discussion of the basic features and benefits of the various LAN options goes beyond the scope of this chapter.

Finding Enough RAM at the Workstation

Probably the single most common problem encountered in implementing a CD-ROM network comes in finding enough free RAM in the workstation to be able to run the CD-ROM applications. A network requires a number of memory resident programs to make it all work--and these all take away from the basic 640K allowed by DOS. A typical workstation on a CD-ROM network will have DOS, ANSI.SYS, network drivers, CD-ROM network device drivers, and Microsoft Extensions--all loaded in memory even before loading the CD-ROM application.

There are now a number of products on the market that help free up precious RAM by loading some of these device drivers or memory resident programs into extended or expanded memory.

The solutions vary, based on the type of workstation and the type of network. For 80386 computers, some memory managers will allow loading certain device drivers and memory resident programs in high memory. For 80286 and 80386 computers, network administrators can often load network drivers into high memory if the computer has at least 1 MB of RAM (and the network drivers have this feature built in). And for any computer with expanded memory, some programs on the market will allow loading device drivers and some memory resident programs into expanded memory. A list of some of these programs appears at the end of this chapter.

Determining the Best CD-ROM Network Solution

Taking a logical approach--following the steps below and asking a few simple questions--can simplify the process of evaluating a CD-ROM network. The steps are as follows: (1) Determine the needs of the CD-ROM applications; (2) Determine the specifications of the local area network hardware and software under consideration; (3) Compare the results of steps 1 and 2 and come up with a list of potential solutions; (4) Compare the additional features required for the CD-ROM network.

1. Determine the Needs of the CD-ROM Applications

For each CD-ROM application you intend to run, you will need to answer the following questions:

- What is the minimum amount of RAM the CD-ROM application requires to run?
- Is the application Microsoft Extensions compatible?
- Does the application make direct calls to either Microsoft Extensions or to the CD-ROM device driver?

2. Determine the Specifications of the Local Area Network

As we discussed in the previous section, some institutions will already have committed themselves to certain brands of local area networks--such as Novell or 3COM--where others can choose the network topology that best meets their needs. Whatever the situation, it is important to obtain the following very basic information for the solutions available:

- Does the solution support direct calls by the application to Microsoft Extensions or to a CD-ROM device driver?
- How much RAM will remain free in the workstation to run the CD-ROM application?

The following is a sample calculation of RAM available:

Table 1.

Total RAM	655,000 bytes
(less)	
DOS	62,000*
ANSI.SYS	2,000
network software	56,000**
CD-ROM network device driver	6,000**
Microsoft Extensions	23,000***
RAM available	506,000

* The size of DOS will vary based on the version and by the number of buffers and other settings in CONFIG.SYS.

** The sizes vary significantly from brand to brand.

*** Includes buffers for one logical CD-ROM drive. If the workstation must have more than one logical CD-ROM drive (e.g. for multiple disc databases), add 8,192 bytes for each additional drive.

3. Compare the Results of the Last Two Steps

The first step should allow drawing up a short list of requirements:

1. Minimum RAM required by the largest application _____
2. Does the application make direct calls to Extensions? _____
3. Does the application make direct calls to the device driver?_____

And for each of the local area network options:

1. Maximum RAM available in the workstation _____
2. Does the application support direct calls to Extensions?_____
3. Does the application support direct calls to the device driver?_____

To state the obvious, to add a network solution to the "acceptable" list, the following should hold true:

- The maximum RAM available in a workstation must equal or exceed the minimum RAM requirements of the largest CD-ROM application.
- If one of the applications performs direct calls to Microsoft Extensions, then the network solution MUST support this.
- If one of the applications performs direct calls to the CD-ROM device driver, then the network solution MUST support this.

4. Compare Additional Features

Once you have compiled your list of "acceptable" network solutions, you can begin by comparing the additional features these solutions may offer. Some of the questions to consider include:

- Will the workstations be used in a public environment?
- Will they require a menu?
- Do you want to prevent users from accessing the DOS prompt?
- Are usage statistics important to you?
- If the network has a large number of workstations, will you want to limit the number of users simultaneously accessing a database?
- Does your institution have the technical expertise to handle the installation and support of the network or do you want the network vendor to supply this expertise?

With the above information gathered and your questions answered, you should be in a position to make an informed decision on the network that will best suit your needs. Selecting a CD-ROM network does not have to present a formidable task. By taking a logical approach of analyzing the needs and weighing the options, you should have the necessary information to find a solution that has the desired features and also meets performance and budget requirements.

Software Resources

CD-ROM Network Products

CD CONNECTION by CBIS, Inc. CD Connection offers a software solution that allows users to access multiple CD-ROM drives across a local area network running Novell Netware or CBIS's Network OS. CD Server comprises the hardware component designed to work with the CD Connection software. The CD Server comes in a tower configuration with up to 7 built-in CD-ROM drives. Users can expand it to include up to 21 CD-ROM players.

The CD Connection software does not require Microsoft Extensions for the individual workstations. Instead Extensions reside in the server. However, the CD Connection software in the workstation handles direct calls to Microsoft Extensions and to the CD-ROM device driver and passes them on to the server.

CD Connection operates on networks running CBIS's own Network OS, Novell's Advanced Netware, MS-Net, and Microsoft's LAN Manager. Other NETBIOS compatible networks may also work but have not been tested.

CD-NET by Meridian Data, Inc. CD-NET by Meridian Data, Inc. provides a combined hardware and software solution for CD-ROM networking. Users can configure Meridian's CD-ROM server with up to 14 CD-ROM drives. The CD-NET software integrates the CD-ROM players on the server into a Novell, 3COM, Unger-mann-Bass, or PC LAN network.

Each CD-ROM player on the CD-NET server appears as a separate logical drive. With this feature the user does not have to use a network command to control the mapping of individual drives. A major drawback to this approach comes from Microsoft Extensions assigning an 8K buffer for each CD-ROM player on the server--this translates to 112K of RAM on a server with 14 CD-ROM drives. To overcome this obstacle, Meridian has announced the upcoming release of database "mounting" software. With the mounting software, each workstation only needs to allocate resources for a single CD-ROM player. The user then "mounts" the database prior to running the retrieval software.

CD-NET comes with a user-friendly menu program to simplify access to the CD-ROM databases. It supports direct calls to Microsoft Extensions and a CD-ROM device driver.

EBSCO's CD-ROM Network by EBSCO Electronic Information. The EBSCO CD-ROM Network, based on the LANtastic Network Operating System and OPTI-NET CD-ROM networking software, provides a very effective and economical solution to CD-ROM networking. It includes an easy-to-use menu system, usage tracking capability, quick installation, and update utilities for CD-ROM application software.

EBSCO uses the LANtastic Network Operating System running on either LANtastic's own proprietary network hardware or on Ethernet hardware. They chose LANtastic because of its RAM efficiency, its ease-of-use, and its economy. It may also support Novell Netware in the future. They chose OPTI-NET to provide the networking capabilities to the CD-ROMs as it supports calls to both Microsoft Extensions and a CD-ROM device driver. With OPTI-NET, virtually any Microsoft Extensions compatible program will run unchanged.

LANtastic by Artisoft, Inc. LANtastic provides a complete network solution that includes the ability to share CD-ROM data across the network. LANtastic comprises a peer-to-peer network, which means that any workstation can share its resources with any other workstation. If an institution has two CD-ROM workstations, it could buy a LANtastic starter kit ($525.00), connect the workstations together, and allow both workstations to access each other's CD-ROM players (all of this provided they have sufficient RAM available to operate as a non-dedicated server and still run a CD-ROM application).

Microsoft Extensions run in the LANtastic server, not in the workstation. LANtastic shares CD-ROM drives as a network hard drive--the workstations link to the CD-ROM database by redirecting a drive letter to the CD-ROM database on the server.

The designers and engineers of LANtastic have done an exceptional job of creating a full-featured network that requires very little RAM to operate. LANtastic only uses 12K of RAM in the workstation, and the server software takes up as little as 32K. The

RAM required for a LANtastic non-dedicated server consumes less than 50K!

Artisoft provides one of the least expensive CD-ROM network solutions on the market by far; however, it has its drawbacks. Because Microsoft Extensions does not run in the workstation, most CD-ROM products performing direct calls to Extensions or the CD-ROM device driver will not run.

MultiPlatter by SilverPlatter, Inc. SilverPlatter's Multiplatter consists of an enhanced version of CD Connection by CBIS. Silverplatter has added value to the CBIS solution by introducing the MultiPlatter Application Manager which includes features such as: a menu system for both CD-ROM and PC based applications, simultaneous usage tracking, statistical reporting, session time-out, session length limits, optional user questionnaire, and monitoring of both workstations and CD-ROMs.

In addition to supporting SilverPlatter CD-ROM databases, MultiPlatter will run most databases from other publishers mastered according to the ISO 9660 standard and which use Microsoft Extensions.

As with CD Connection, MultiPlatter comes with Microsoft Extensions emulation software which runs in the workstation. This allows databases which communicate directly with Extensions or a CD-ROM device driver to run unchanged.

MultiPlatter includes a feature that allows the network manager to set the maximum number of simultaneous users for each database. This feature can also serve to enforce the database license restrictions of some information providers.

MultiPlatter operates on networks running CBIS's Network OS, Novell's Advanced Netware, MS-Net, and Microsoft's LAN Manager. Other NETBIOS compatible networks may also work but have not been tested.

OPTI-NET by Online Computer Products, Inc. OPTI-NET software is designed to provide multi-user access, through a local area network, to CD-ROM databases. OPTI-NET will operate with most networks fully supporting the NETBIOS protocol or the Novell IPX/SPX protocol and will support up to 100 simultaneous users per CD-ROM server. It will accommodate use of up to nine CD-ROM servers on one network; and each CD-ROM server can support up to 64 CD-ROM players.

OPTI-NET server software can run in either a dedicated or non-dedicated mode. In theory, the non-dedicated mode allows any workstation on the network to operate as an optical server. However, in practice, this is often not the case due to the memory requirements of the OPTI-NET server software.

Databases mounted on the CD-ROM server receive logical names. Workstations access CD-ROM databases by application name, eliminating the need to preassign drive letters or numbers. After opening a database, the OPTI-NET program operates completely transparently--the CD-ROM application functions as if it were accessing a local CD-ROM drive. The OPTI-NET software supports multiple disc databases as well as the more typical single disc database.

OPTI-NET comes in both an IPX/SPX and NETBIOS version. The IPX version will run on any network running the Novell Advanced Netware software. The NETBIOS version will run on most other networks--those definitely supported include: Microsoft LAN Manager, MS-NET, LANtastic, and 3-COM Ethernet.

Products for Freeing Conventional Memory

LANspace by LAN Systems, Inc. This product assists 80286 and 80386 workstations with at least 1 MB of RAM on a Novell network. LANspace allows loading into high memory (memory between 640K and 1024K [i.e. 1MB]) either Novell's IPX or NET3 programs. This will free up to 40K of RAM. LANspace will not work for 8088 (IBM PC & XT compatibles) or 80286 computers with only 640K RAM.

386-To-The-Max by Qualitas, Inc. If you have an 80386 computer with at least 1 MB of RAM, this memory manager will allow you to run device drivers and resident programs such as Microsoft Extensions and network drivers in high DOS memory. Some restrictions on the size of the resident program apply; however, it might recover up to 100K of RAM.

MOVE'EM by Qualitas, Inc. This program loader brings high DOS program loading capabilities to any IBM compatible system configured with a fully hardware compatible EMS 4.0 memory board or that has either a NEAT or AT/386 CHIPSET from Chips and Technologies. MOVE'EM allows loading device drivers and TSR programs into high DOS memory, freeing 60K or more of conventional RAM.

QEMM by Quarterdeck Office Systems. This memory manager, also designed solely for the 80386, can load device drivers and resident programs into high DOS memory. It should be possible to handle DOS buffers as well as network drivers and Microsoft Extensions. As with 386-To-The-Max, some restrictions apply on the size of programs that it can load into high memory. However, it can recover up to 100K of RAM.

QRAM by Quarterdeck Office Systems. With this product (pronounced CRAM), you can load resident programs into expanded memory. Virtually any workstation with EMS memory can use this solution. You can add expanded memory cards to IBM PC and XT compatible machines as well as to 80286 machines. With QRAM it should be possible to load the network drivers and Microsoft Extensions in EMS memory, again freeing up to 60K of RAM or more.

Notes

1. Novell file server must be dedicated and cannot run normal DOS programs such as a CD-ROM server application.

2. If insufficient available RAM at the workstation becomes a problem, one has a number of potential solutions. Refer to "Finding Enough RAM at the Workstation" on p.26.

3
Hardware Options
Ka-Neng Au

Apart from the disk operating system software, Microsoft CD-ROM Extensions, network operating system, and special device drivers discussed in the previous chapter, a CD-ROM LAN requires several hardware components. These include the network itself, computer workstations, the file server and/or the CD-ROM server, and CD-ROM drives. This chapter will discuss some of the options available for each of these hardware components when designing a CD-ROM LAN.

PC-Based Network Architectures

The most common networks in use today include Ethernet, Token Ring, and ARCnet, as discussed in the previous chapter. Ethernet consists of both a network and a transmission protocol developed jointly by the Xerox Corporation and Digital Equipment Corporation. It conforms to the IEEE 802.3 contention access LAN standard. Typically, it has a bus topology although it can also be configured as a star. It has a data transfer rate or operating speed of 10 Mbps (megabits per second) regardless of the topology. Ethernet networks will operate over coaxial (both ThinNet and standard coax), fiber optic, or twisted pair cables. Many vendors make network interface cards (NICs) for Ethernet networks.

The Token Ring network, developed by the International Business Machines Corporation (IBM), conforms to the IEEE 802.5 token-passing ring protocol standard. It has a physical-star, logical-ring topology. Its data transfer rate is 4 Mbps or 16 Mbps, depending on the NIC chosen. One forms a Token Ring network by linking NICs to a multistation access unit (MAU) with the appropriate twisted pair adapter cable. The IBM cabling system includes three common options: Type 1 (two individually shielded twisted pairs); Type 2 (two individually shielded pairs and four unshielded pairs); Type 3 (unshielded twisted pair). Types 1 and 2 can work in either a 4 or 16 Mbps network, while Type 3 is only recommended for 4 Mbps Token Ring networks.

ARCnet (Attached Resources Computing) was developed by Datapoint Corporation. One can configure it in a star or a bus topology. The IEEE does not endorse its token-passing protocol; but the network remains a popular choice because of its low cost and versatility. Its data transfer rate is 2.5 Mbps, and it will operate with coaxial or twisted pair cable. As with Ethernet, many vendors make NICs for ARCnet networks.

Workstations

Figure 1. *Key to LAN Configurations.*

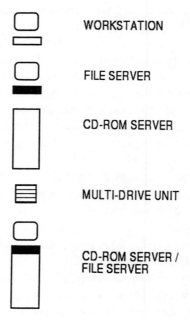

The microcomputers used as workstations in a LAN tend to consist of 8086 or 80286-based machines, with 640KB of RAM, oftentimes a hard disk, and a network interface card (NIC) linking the microcomputer to the network. Choosing a public-access workstation resembles choosing a microcomputer for any other purpose: the key factors come down to reliability, vendor support, and price. The make or model seldom matters, unless your institution has special volume discounts with specific manufacturers. On the other hand, color monitors do matter, since most software packages take advantage of color in order to enhance legibility of screen displays.

The hard disk also becomes necessary in a CD-ROM workstation because many CD-ROM search software packages require loading from a local drive rather than downloading from the file server. You may also need more than 640KB of RAM if your networking software leaves you with insufficient memory to load the search software. As computer prices fall, the possibility that you will choose 80386- or 80386SX-based machines will rise.

File Servers and CD-ROM Servers

A typical LAN requires a microcomputer dedicated to the operation of the network. This microcomputer, called the file server, usually has a fast microprocessor (e.g. 80386, or at least a faster one than the workstation's microprocessor) and a 30 to 60MB hard disk. In addition, in order to run the network operating system, the file server also requires more memory (1-4MB) than the workstations. Any memory left over can serve disk caching to offset the relative slowness of the CD-ROM drives.

The server determines, in part, the speed of the network. Relevant factors include: the type of microprocessor, the clock rate of the microprocessor, the architecture of the input/output bus and the memory bus, and the access rate of the hard disk.[1] A microcomputer with an 80386-25 MHz chip and MicroChannel bus architecture will definitely provide faster network access than a PC or AT class machine could.

However, no typical CD-ROM LAN exists. Instead of a separate file server, a CD-ROM LAN might only have a CD-ROM server. It might have both a file server and a CD-ROM server, or no server at all. There are, in fact, at least five distinct configurations of CD-ROM LANs: Types 1, 2, 3a, and 3b consist of centralized networks with some sort of server. Type 4 comprises a decentralized network with no dedicated server.

CD-ROM LAN Configurations

Figure 2. *Type 1: CD-ROM Server Only.*[2]

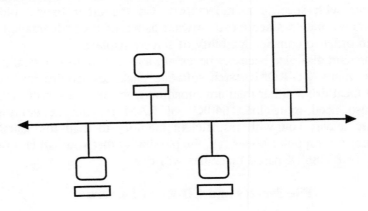

In this configuration, a CD-ROM server is attached to a small network with perhaps three to five workstations. This is a network-aware storage device (with multiple CD-ROM drives) which resembles a high-end microcomputer CPU that stands upright, such as the IBM PS/2 Model 60 tower. A typical example of this configuration is Meridian Data's CD Net system in an Ethernet network, which uses only the IPX communications protocol and not the whole Novell NetWare network operating system (NOS). Another example would comprise a CD Net tower in an Artisoft LANtastic network, using the LANtastic NOS.

Figure 3. *Type 2: CD-ROM Server and File Server.*[3]

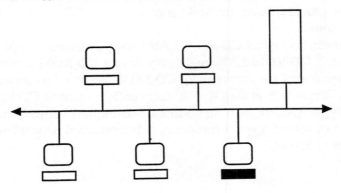

This configuration basically expands on the Type 1 CD-ROM LAN. It adds a file server to accomodate the full network operating system and to manage additional network services such as centralized printing. Alternatively, one could attach a CD-ROM server to an existing network which has a file server. The file server would then control just the network while the the CD-ROM server would manage the CD-ROMs. One would install controller card(s) for one or more multidrive units in this microcomputer rather than in the file server. Type 2 networks typically support four to twenty workstations. Examples include both the Meridian Data CD Net system and the CBIS CD Server/CD Connection combination.

Figure 4. *Type 3a: File Server/CD-ROM Server Combination.*[4, 5]

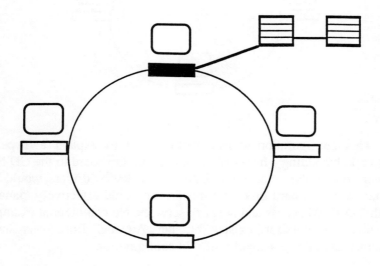

This configuration takes an existing LAN and adds multiple CD-ROM drives to the file server along with the CD-ROM controller card(s). The NOS and the CD-ROM device drivers for network access would be installed on its hard disk, along with optional memory management software. In effect, this file server would manage the LAN and all network operations, such as printing and messaging, as well as manage access to the CD-ROM drives attached to it (McQueen calls this an optical server).[6] Typically, a Type 3a network could support up to 10 workstations per server. As an example, the

Opti-Net software and optical storage units (OSU) from Online Products Corporation are designed for a Type 3a network.

Figure 5. *Type 3b: CD-ROM Server/File Server Combination.*[7]

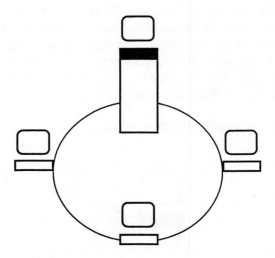

This configuration shows another way to expand a Type 1 network, by adding a hard disk, monitor, and keyboard to the CD Net tower. As in Type 3a, the full NOS and device drivers would be installed on the hard disk, and this server would effectively manage both CD-ROM access and network services. No commercial example of this configuration exists yet; but Au and Borisovets have demonstrated the practicality of this configuration.

Figure 6. *Type 4: No Dedicated Server.*[8]

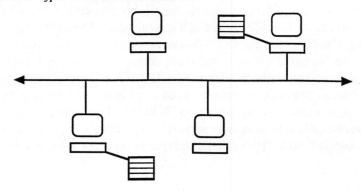

This configuration allows connecting several CD-ROM workstations to one another so as to allow each one to have access to the CD-ROM drives attached to another workstation. It has no dedicated file server or CD-ROM server. Each workstation may or may not have CD-ROM drives attached. The LANtastic network hardware and software products enable relatively easy setup of Type 4 networks. Another example would involve using Novell's Entry Level System I (ELS I) NOS in non-dedicated mode and adding Fresh Technology Group's MAP Assist to provide the CD-ROM access.

CD-ROM Servers (Towers)

Using a CD-ROM server as the primary storage device for a CD-ROM LAN offers several advantages: single controller, single power supply, single unit to administer, compact storage, and security. Prospective buyers currently have two available choices here: CD Net from Meridian Data, Inc. and CD Server from CBIS.

While the previous model of the CD Net tower only held up to five drives (an expansion chassis with no microprocessor had room for an additional six drives), the latest CD Net towers can accomodate up to 14 CD-ROM drives. The new design features include an improved air filtering system and a lockable front door that restricts access to the drives and power switch.

Model 214 contains an 80286 chip running at 12 MHz; Model 314 has a 20 MHz, 80386 microprocessor. Both models come with 1 MB of RAM (expandable to 8 MB) and a 1.44 MB floppy drive. Users can configure both for an Ethernet, a Token Ring, or an ARCnet network. The drives have a 350 millisecond average access time; the SCSI controller card also holds a proprietary chip with part of the CD Net software on it as firmware.

The CBIS CD Server resembles the old CD Net tower in design. This CD Server has room for up to seven CD-ROM drives controlled by a SCSI adapter. Two of the three models available come equipped with microprocessors: the CD Server/286 has a 12 MHz 80286 chip and 2 MB memory on the motherboard; the CD Server/386 has a 20 MHz 80386 chip and 4 MB RAM. These two come with a 1.2 MB floppy drive. The expansion chassis model has no microprocessor or floppy drive; it also holds up to seven CD-ROM drives.

The expansion chassis can serve to increase the number of drives connected to the CD Server. You can also connect it to an existing

(286 or 386) workstation on your network. The CD Server is designed for use with CBIS CD Connection software. This combined CBIS solution will accomodate up to twenty-one drives per network file server.

SilverPlatter markets an almost complete networked CD-ROM system based on the CBIS system under the name MultiPlatter. This product comes with the CD Server/286, Ethernet NICs, an NOS, Microsoft CD-ROM Extensions, and special MultiPlatter software to manage the CD-ROMs over the network. Additional drives or servers are available; but SilverPlatter does not provide the workstations or the Ethernet cables.

Multidrive Units

One can also daisy-chain more than one player or multidrive units together, with one or more CD-ROM controller cards in a file server, to achieve the same effect as the tower units. Apart from the numerous vendors that manufacture single CD-ROM players, at least five companies market multidrive units: CD-Plus (CDP), CD-ROM, Inc. (CDR), OCLC, Online Computer Products, Inc. (OCP), and Todd Enterprises (Todd). Table 1 summarizes some of their features.

Table 1.

Make	Model	Avg access (in ms)	Interface type	# Drives/ Controller
CDP	MultiDrive	450	SCSI/Hitachi	8
CDR	Texel	430	SCSI	6
OCLC	CDR-3600	450	Hitachi	8
OCP	OSU	350	SCSI	8
Todd	TCDR 3004	450	SCSI/Hitachi	8
Todd	TCDR 4004	450	Hitachi	8

The multidrive units from all five companies have a similar design. Each one can contain up to four drives stacked above each other in a case. However, several models have distinctive features: the OCLC unit has a handle; the CDP MultiDrive and Todd TCDR 4004 have a front panel lock; the CDR unit holds up to six drives. CDP, OCLC, and Todd use Hitachi drives exclusively; the other two firms use either Toshiba or Sony drives.

Except for the Todd TCDR 3004, each of the above units has its own power supply. This means that only one power outlet is necessary. If you want to daisy-chain individual CD-ROMs, you need as many outlets as you have drives.

Other Devices

Consumers currently have two very different kinds of jukeboxes to choose from. The Pioneer CD-ROM Minichanger holds up to six CD-ROMs in a magazine cartridge; the Voyager from Next Technology of the United Kingdom can accomodate as many as 270 discs. However, the Minichanger is not really suitable for use in a networked environment. Typically, more than one user will want to have access to the resources on a LAN. And typically, each CD-ROM user will want to have access to a different database. With only one read head, the Minichanger would have to continually switch discs in order to satisfy the users. Disc changing takes about seven seconds.

On the other hand, users can configure the Voyager to have up to eight CD-ROM drives. It will switch discs in about five seconds and load them into one of the drives. The device is compatible with Ethernet networks in a Novell NetWare or Microsoft LAN Manager environment.[9]

The market also has available two devices designed for non-PC-based LANs. These devices permit access to PC-based CD-ROM products from a minicomputer-based network. Logicraft's CD-Ware consists of a network DOS server that attaches directly to a Digital Equipment Corporation VAX/VMS network via an Ethernet NIC. It allows workstations and terminals on the network to have access to as many as 16 CD-ROM drives. Each device contains an 80386 chip and can accomodate up to 16 MB of RAM to support a maximum of 16 simultaneous users.

Virtual Microsystems make a hardware/software system called the V-Server/Gateway which acts as a gateway from a VAX network to a PC-based LAN. Each V-Server device holds up to four 80286-based boards called client processors. Each of these client processors has 1 MB of RAM and is paired with its own NIC to connect with the PC-based LAN. The PC-based LAN must incorporate the CD-ROM drives to allow users on the VAX network to have access to CD-ROMs. In other words, up to four simultaneous VAX users per V-Server/Gateway system can access an existing PC-based CD-ROM LAN.[10]

Future Developments

Given the continuously evolving state of computer technology, new products are bound to appear on the market by the time this book appears in print. For example, jukeboxes for erasable optical discs and write-once, read-many (WORM) discs have come on the market. Their design may affect how future jukeboxes for CD-ROMs will be built. As the installed base of CD-ROM titles and drives grows, and as more and more sites pursue the networking of their CD-ROM resources, we can expect end-users to voice their opinions for new hardware products that will meet their needs.

Mail-order Suppliers of LAN Products

Black Box Corp.
P.O. Box 12800
Pittsburgh, PA15241-0800
412-746- 5530

South Hills Electronics
760 Beechnut Dr
Pittsburg, PA 15205-9983
800-245-6215

CABLExpress
500 East Brighton Ave
Syracuse, NY 13210
315-476-3100

Westcon Associates, Inc.
150 Main St
Eastchester, NY 10707
800-527-9516

Vendors of CD-ROM Equipment

Artisoft
575 East River Rd
Tucson, AZ 85704
602-293-6363

CBIS
5875 Peachtree Industrial Blvd
Building 100, Suite 170
Norcross, GA 30092
404-446-3337

Bureau of Electronic Publishing
141 New Road
Parsippany, NJ 07054
201-808-2700

CD Plus
951 Amsterdam Ave, Suite 2C
New York, NY 10025
212-932-1485

CD ROM, Inc.
1667 Cole Blvd, Suite 400
Golden, CO 80401
303-231-9373

Fresh Technology Group
1478 North Tech Blvd,
Suite 101
Gilbert, AZ 85234
602-497-420

Logicraft
22 Cotton Rd
Nashua, NH 03063
603-880-0300

Meridian Data, Inc.
5615 Scotts Valley Dr
Scotts Valley, CA 95066
408-438-3100

Next Technology Corp. Ltd
St Johns Innovation Centre
Cambridge CB4 4WS England
0223-421-180

OCLC
6565 Frantz Rd
Dublin, OH 43017
800-848-5878 ext. 5040

Online Products Corp.
20251 Century Blvd
Germantown, MD 20874
301-428-3700

Pioneer Communications of
America
600 East Crescent Ave
Upper Saddle River, NJ 07458
201-327-6400

SilverPlatter Information Inc.
One Newton Executive Park
Newton Lower Falls, MA
02162
800-343-0064 / 617-969-5554

Todd Enterprises
224-49 67th Ave 1825
Bayside, NY 11364
718-343-1040

Virtual Microsystems, Inc.
S. Grant St, Suite 700
San Mateo, CA 94402
415-573-9596

Notes

1. Michael Day, "LAN Times server showdown," *LAN Times* 7:8 (August, 1990): 83.
2. Types 1 and 2 are discussed in: James Jay Morgan, "The Indiana University School of Medicine Library Meridian CD-ROM Network," paper presented at Networking CD-ROM Technologies Preconference, Library and Information Technology Association, Chicago, June 22, 1990. For another example of a Type 1 CD-ROM LAN, *see* Ka-Neng Au and Natalie Borisovets, "The changing LANdscape of undergraduate research: The Rutgers-

Newark experience," in *Public Access CD-ROMs in Libraries: Case Studies*, edited by L. Stewart, K. Chiang and B. Coons (Westport, CT: Meckler, 1990): 228. [Cluster 3]

3. The Type 2 CD-ROM LAN corresponds to Configuration One in: John Rutherford, "Improving CD-ROM management through networking," *CD-ROM Professional* 3:5 (September, 1990): 22.
4. Ibid. [Configuration Two]
5. Au and Borisovets, 226-27. [Cluster 1]
6. Howard McQueen, "Networking CD-ROMs." *CD-ROM EndUser* 1:11 (March, 1990): 92-93.
7. Au and Borisovets, 227. [Cluster 2]
8. Rutherford, 22. [Configuration Three]
9. Nancy Melin Nelson, "On the cutting edge: Next Technology's CD-ROM jukebox," *CD-ROM Librarian* 4:9 (October, 1989): 22-24.
10. Paula Musich, "Gateway lets VAXes access LAN data," *PC Week* 5 (August 28, 1989): 58.

For Further Reading

Elshami, Ahmed M. *CD-ROM Technology for Information Managers*. Chicago: American Library Association, 1990.

Lazzaro, Joseph. "Networking with optical disk technology." *LAN Technology* 6:4 (April, 1990): 43-48.

Madron, Thomas. *Local Area Networks: The Next Generation*. 2nd ed. New York: John Wiley, 1990.

Thompson, M. Keith and Kimberly Maxwell. "Building workgroup solutions: Networking CD-ROMs." *PC Magazine* 9:4 (February 27, 1990): 237-60.

4
Considerations for the System Manager

Joyce Demmitt and Norma Hill

Overview

The decision to network CD-ROM databases changes and enhances the delivery of information within an organization; but it does so at considerable cost. To determine whether networking CD-ROM databases is appropriate, one needs to take a careful and thorough look at the organization's goals and financial resources.

Five initial views of the organization start the process:

1. A review of the long range plan to determine where CD-ROM databases fit.
2. Consideration of the year's goals and objectives to set a reasonable implementation timetable.
3. Contemplation of the clientele.
4. An examination of staff workload to determine who will be involved in the project.
5. A scrutiny of the financial resources available to cover start-up costs.

If the organization determines that it should offer a variety of CD-ROM databases to its clientele and that it has adequate funding to support their introduction, then examining the feasibility of networking is appropriate. This should prove a cost effective solution in the long run.

The next chapter will discuss the alternatives to networking in greater depth; but obvious alternatives include the single workstation supporting a single database or the single workstation supporting multiple databases. Single workstations have numerous disadvantages if the databases get heavy use. They include: long lines, time limitations, booking systems, staff constantly changing discs to accommodate patron requests, and the possibility of damage to or loss of the discs. All require staff time and staff monitoring and would hinder optimum use of the databases.

Preplanning

As part of preplanning for a LAN, the administrative planning team should consider carefully its clientele, with a number of questions in mind. Are the patrons computer literate? Will they get served from a single location or multiple locations? Will individual users be allowed to dial in to the LAN? What about training for the users and publicity for the services? The answer to each of the questions impacts directly on the budget needed to implement a LAN.

These answers also determine the configuration of the LAN. A network located in a single building rather than in multiple buildings is much simpler to configure and constitutes a local area network rather than a wide area network (WAN). University campuses, in particular, might prefer implementing wide area networks for access by students and faculty from a variety of locations. This chapter will discuss only the issues related to implementing a LAN. However, many of the considerations would also apply to the contemplation of a WAN.

Budget Considerations

When budgeting for a LAN, one must include the following costs in the initial budget: consultant fees (if needed), personnel costs (LAN Administrator) and any other personnel costs associated with LAN maintenance, hardware (both workstation and LAN hardware), software, wiring, furniture, and product costs (including any networking fees). Planners should also consider ongoing costs for subscription renewal and any support materials needed for upkeep of the workstations. Funding should be allocated in each budget year for enhancements to the LAN as technology improves and/or changes.

Here are some basic budget figures which could serve as a financial planning guide:

1. Consultant--negotiate the cost as a flat fee or as an hourly fee to be determined by what you ask the consultant to do. Figure on approximately $5000 total or $100 per hour.
2. LAN Administrator--$ 30,000 per annum if a new position is created.
3. Wiring--$1500 minimum; but cost depends on the type of cable (coax, twisted pair, etc.) and network card chosen (Arcnet, Ethernet, etc.). Distance from network hub to workstations also impacts cost.
4. Network server and software--$5,700.
5. File Server, software and 3 four-drive CD-ROM units--$11,300.
6. Workstations--$3,500 each.
7. Furniture--$1,000 per station.
8. Products--$12,000 for 8-12 databases, depending on individual cost of each database.
9. Ongoing supplies (ribbon, paper, etc.)--$2,000 per year.

Developing the Request for Proposal

The planning team should now determine the scope of the LAN: how many workstations, how many products; whether minimal staff involvement with LAN upkeep and maintenance is desired. These decisions will determine the qualifications of the LAN administrator, whether additional technical staff is needed, and, to some extent, the type of LAN to be implemented. Turnkey LANs such as a SilverPlatter's require less technical knowledge on the part of staff; but they limit, to some extent, the ability to enhance the LAN as new products emerge. The vendor will implement enhancements when customers generate sufficient demand or when the market dictates change.

The extent of staff involvement in working with the LAN becomes the key to all other decisions. If you decide to build your own LAN, then you should include the following in the request for proposal (RFP):

- A detailed overview of the LAN which includes whether users will be allowed to download or to print out search results, whether there will be remote workstations, etc.
- Configuration of network server (if needed)
- Configuration of the CD-ROM file server

- Network interface card (will determine type of wiring needed)
- Workstation configuration, including any peripheral equipment such as printers. Consider both floppy and hard drive requirements, also 386 machines in order to take advantage of high memory.
- CD-ROM drive requirements
- Software requirements
- Security issues
- Warranty and maintenance requirements
- Future considerations
- Network support

If the organization employs a very knowledgeable information systems manager, then it may not need a consultant. However, it would be wise to hire a consultant during the planning and implementation stage of the project. Many incompatibilities could surface with the hardware and software which would require an ability to troubleshoot both hardware and software. It is also extremely important to negotiate return of any products that do not perform as expected. The organization could expect the consultant hired to do the following:

- Develop the request for proposal
- Review the responses to the request for proposal with the planning team
- Help with the resulting purchase orders
- Oversee the wiring
- Install the LAN hardware and software
- Test the LAN for reliability
- Document the file setup
- Train the LAN administrator and LAN staff

LAN Administrator

The organization must appoint a LAN administrator to oversee the operation of the LAN on a day-to-day basis. Qualifications for this position are important to the success of the project. Minimum qualifications include:

- Knowledge of microcomputer hardware/software
- Working knowledge of MS-DOS
- Previous experience with on-line searching, in particular familiarity with Boolean logic
- Working knowledge of the LAN software selected or the ability to learn quickly
- Technical ability (needed to install, troubleshoot new software, CD-ROMs, etc.)
- Training ability
- Ability to interact with vendors and technical support staff
- Planning skills
- Commitment to and enthusiasm for new and changing technologies

Responsibilities

The majority of the items listed above become integral to the position. The LAN administrator also must keep administration abreast of any LAN difficulties (recurring hardware problems, problems with products on the LAN, or problems with the LAN software itself.) The administrator should have responsibility for statistics and should have the ability to provide administration with a profile of the users of the LAN and the products most heavily used.

The LAN administrator serves as the system trainer and demonstrator. Presentation skills are important and the ability to discuss the makeup of the LAN with outside contacts is necessary.

The LAN administrator also translates manuals into understandable instructions for staff and public.

Other Staff Requirements

The LAN administrator will not be available 24 hours per day to troubleshoot and operate the LAN. In planning, it is important to consider additional staffing requirements, not only to monitor LAN operations but to staff the LAN if it serves as an extension of the reference desk.

Product Selection and Costs

Costs of CD-ROM databases vary greatly from a few hundred dollars to thousands. In planning, one should select potential products and factor prices into both initial and ongoing costs. One then contacts each publisher for pricing and should mention network size. Costs vary. Some publishers allow networking their product without additional fees. Others charge a per workstation fee. Publishers' stance may also vary if the organization includes remote access to the network in the implementation plan.

It is important to establish a timetable for implementation of the LAN. Without a specific timetable, it is easy to become lost in the process of investigating and testing products.

Always bear in mind the institution's LAN clientele. That, along with the budget, will guide product selection. The number of CD-ROM products continues to grow at a phenomenal rate. With so many products on the market, one can very easily get swept up in the excitement of individual products and lose sight of clients. It is important to keep in mind a balanced collection unless one purchases for a very specialized library.

One can find product reviews regularly in each of the following periodicals. Other traditional library reviewing sources contain information on CD-ROMs; but they do not cover them nearly as extensively.

CD-ROM EndUser. DDRI, Incorporated, 510 North Washington Street, Suite 401, Falls Church, VA 22046-3537; free.

CD-ROM Librarian. Meckler Corporation, 11 Ferry Lane West, Westport, CT 06880; $79.50 per year.

CD-ROM Professional. (Formerly *Laserdisk Professional*). Pemberton Press, Inc., 11 Tannery Lane, Weston, CT 06883; $86 per year.

Computers in Libraries. Meckler Corporation, 11 Ferry Lane West, Westport, CT 06880; $72.50 per year.

Database: the Magazine of Database Reference and Review. Database, 11 Tannery Lane, Weston, CT 06883; $85 per year.

After identifying databases which appear to meet clients' needs, one should then review them thoroughly, answering several questions:

1. Has the publisher enhanced an already existing print product with useful search capabilities?

2. Does the value of the new product justify the additional cost over the print version?

3. How easy is it to use this product successfully?

4. Does it have clear documentation, both for use and for installation?

5. How old is the data included in the product?

6. How often does it get updated?

7. Do the brochures talk about enhancements: sound/animation/video?

Some vendors seem to have little commitment to updating existing products. Currency is critical if you plan to retain a product on your network.

Reading a publisher's brochure will undoubtedly not reveal all the information essential before making a purchase. Sending a specific letter such as the following is most beneficial.

Sample Letter

Dear   ;

X Library is developing a local area network for the public featuring a variety of CD-ROM databases housed behind the scenes. Once we complete our LAN, we plan an extensive publicity campaign. We would like to include NAME OF PRODUCT on our LAN. Please answer several specific questions for us.

1. May we use NAME OF PRODUCT in a network environment?

2. What is your network fee structure? Please be sure to include the charge for non-profit organizations.

3. Is a site license available?

4. Would any other fees be required in addition to our site license fee?

5. If you are still considering the networking question, when do you anticipate a decision?

6. May we provide remote access to your product? Is use from another library location billed as an additional workstation charge?

7. May we provide dial-in access to the public, either during or after regular library hours?

8. Exactly how much free RAM (Random Access Memory) does NAME OF PRODUCT require?

9. What hardware is required to run NAME OF PRODUCT?

10. Does NAME OF PRODUCT allow users to print and download data?

11. Please include information on the exact number of compact discs we will receive with each available year of your product.

12. How often will we receive updates and how many discs will we receive with each update/edition?

13. Since we are setting up a LAN containing products from a variety of manufacturers, how long a test period may we have for NAME OF PRODUCT in order to see whether or not it is compatible with other products on our LAN?

14. Do you have an 800 number and a technical support staff familiar with CD-ROM Local Area Networks so that our LAN administrator can talk with someone specific if s/he encounters problems installing new releases?

Please respond by X date so that we may begin purchasing our CD-ROM databases. Please include a current product brochure with your reply.

Sincerely,

Providing a fairly short response time is important so you can make selections and begin testing on the network.

Once responses arrive, determine which products to begin testing. At this point, it is important to test each product in a network environment. Time spent becomes a major cost factor if a product under consideration functions quite well in a standalone mode, but then does not run reliably on the network.

Be sure to order only as many products at a time as you can test during the given periods. If the LAN administrator works alone on this phase of the project, be certain he or she has sufficient time to test the full capabilities of each product before needing to move on to others. It is important to remember, however, the need to install several products on the network at the same time, to ensure their compatibility with each other.

This is an excellent time to begin to involve other staff with the LAN. They can assist with testing products and pointing out difficulties.

After completing the testing phase, make final decisions, bearing in mind initial costs along with annual renewals. You should also keep in mind that prices so readily published for a CD-ROM product generally apply to the standalone version, not the network version. Because networking is still relatively new for CD-ROM products, you should enter into written agreements with CD-ROM publishers before paying for any products.

At this point, it is also vital to consider staff knowledge of and comfort with this technology. Factor in training time for staff on search strategies in general; on specifics for each product you add to your LAN; and, if the technology is very new for them, on Boolean logic. Be aware that, given the wide range of search software which accompanies products, this individual product training consumes a large amount of time.

Acquisitions and Cataloging

If you house the CD-ROMs behind the scenes, you may not need to catalog them. Clients will have access through the LAN; and the LAN menu will tell them what is available. If clients have access to the CD-ROMs themselves, it would be wise to catalog, process, and affix some type of security to them.

If the library has an online catalog, an OPAC, it would be a good idea to include a producer/title/subject entry for each product, including the years of coverage so that clients will know to look for these items on the LAN. This approach may be especially important if the LAN includes sources which get consulted frequently through online searching in the library. For example, many clients who had previously requested online searching may be well satisfied to have direct access to products such as *ERIC* and *MEDLINE* on CD-ROM.

Training

Training is a vital component in the successful implementation of a LAN. Staff must understand the purpose of the LAN, how it fits into the library's service plan, and how to use it. Train staff in the operation and maintenance of the LAN and in how to work successfully with the LAN and the clients. Train the clients so their searches yield the most complete results possible.

LAN Operation and Maintenance

We have already discussed the responsibilities of the LAN administrator. The ability to train is key. Since this person will not be available at all times, other staff must be knowledgeable about and comfortable with bringing up the system, taking it down, cleaning the CD-ROM drives, and basic troubleshooting. Having a group of people who all share these responsibilities offers a good way to increase commitment to the system.

Write simple instructions for each of these areas and review them verbally. Staff then need time to practice and should be assigned a regular schedule for these tasks.

A basic troubleshooting guide should include what to do if:

- a screen or keyboard freezes
- printer paper jams
- printing is too light
- you can't connect to a particular product
- the entire system freezes

LAN Product Knowledge and Public Interface

Staff often become the key to a successful public interface with the network, particularly if clients are unfamiliar with or reticent about technology. Staff must be well-versed on the capabilities of the network, general search strategies, and the particulars of each product installed.

Training must include information on how to start up and shut down the system and who is responsible for each, menu screens and their function, and printing and downloading specifics.

Staff need to spend a good deal of time on Boolean logic and general search strategies for each of the databases. It is usually helpful to have staff work in small groups with someone knowledgeable about the database during the training session. Allow ample opportunity for questions.

After this introductory session, staff should have time to work individually or in small groups on actual questions so that they can have first-hand knowledge of each database in the system. Rushing this aspect of the training can result in major problems later if staff find themselves incapable of assisting patrons in their searches. One might find it helpful to delineate a maximum amount of time to be spent on the questions so that staff do not become consumed with the project. When staff complete the question sheets, it is a good idea to route them through their supervisors and the LAN administrator so that these individuals can assess areas of need for additional training.

Perhaps a month, or at least several weeks later, bring staff together again to review the questions. Go over any additional fine points about the system and each of the databases and be certain that staff understand the implementation timetable and all LAN procedures. Questions regarding possible user time limits, age limits, and printing limits may well present a concern and the LAN administrator needs to be prepared to deal with each.

Training the Public

Knowledge of the library's clientele will determine the type and frequency of training offered. If the public has little computer expertise, it may require lengthy orientation sessions, similar to those conducted for staff. If, on the other hand, clientele have a high level of computer literacy, a simple introduction to the mechanics of the LAN may suffice.

Decide on the amount of written documentation the library will provide. Often the "Users' Manuals" seem designed to cloud, rather than convey, information. A simple users' guide developed in-house can offer general database information and basic search strategies for each product. CD-ROM products usually provide on-screen help. That may suffice for many people. But for those who want more or who find more comfort with the printed page, a users' guide developed by library staff may prove most helpful.

Security Issues

The Network

Depending on the library setting, one may find passwords for using the network quite useful, particularly if the network has applications software available along with access to the CD-ROMs. If the network offers dial-up access, passwords become essential to prevent intruders from readily accessing the network.

The CD-ROMs

If you keep the CD-ROMs themselves behind the scenes, you can handle their security fairly easily. Limit access to the room which houses the file server. Instruct staff on how to handle the discs properly when they clean them and the drives.

Search Software

Patrons may try to access the search software for individual products. If each workstation has its own hard drive, you can install all search software for the network on each drive. Therefore, if anyone tampers with a particular product, you would need to restore only that workstation's hard drive.

DOS

Hackers relish the challenge of breaking into DOS. A good deal of the menu software available offers safeguards in this area. Direct Access, produced by Delta Technologies in Eau Claire, Wisconsin, offers safeguards regarding access to both file maintenance and DOS. Many menu systems provide elaborate safeguards at the expense of ease of installation and with extensive use of passwords in order to access the system. When using such a program, it becomes important to select one which does not discourage general use by clients.

Viruses

Because viruses of all types are so widespread and so easy to introduce into systems, one should purchase virus detection software which a staff member would use daily on each workstation. This type of simple detection device may save countless hours later if someone manages to infect the network.

Hardware/Printers

Damage to computer hardware and printers may more often result from heavy use rather than from deliberate abuse by clients. Factor anticipated usage into the RFP so that any equipment purchased will be able to withstand institutional, rather than in-home use.

Consider warranties and repair contracts as well. On-site repair is ideal. If you must send equipment out for repairs, the loan of replacement equipment is often helpful so that the LAN can continue in full operation.

Conclusion

Many factors influence the decision to network CD-ROM databases. The willingness to take risks, albeit carefully calculated risks, becomes a major consideration. Thorough research is essential. As experienced CD-ROM LAN developers, we think that proper planning, careful implementation, a good sense of humor, along with a well-trained staff will ensure a successful network and a satisfied clientele.

5
Alternatives to CD-ROM Networks
Norman Desmarais

There's no doubt about it. Implementing a CD-ROM network presents an expensive proposition. Initial start-up costs are quite high. However, incremental costs for adding extra workstations or products remain relatively low. Networking may not present a feasible option for a small library with only a few databases in optical format. On the other hand, large libraries which make heavy use of particular databases may wish to have a more efficient alternative than CD-ROM. This chapter examines these options.

Dedicated Workstations

The first alternative to consider in implementing a CD-ROM search system involves whether or not to dedicate a particular workstation to a specific product. This approach has benefits in an environment that uses few CD-ROM databases or for a product that gets heavy use by a limited number of clients. The disadvantage comes in the relatively high costs of dedicating a microcomputer and CD-ROM drive to a single application or product.

Very heavy usage of this kind of product may warrant an additional copy or subscription. The decision maker needs to determine the break-even point and decide whether the incremental costs of purchasing an additional copy or subscription and another workstation and CD-ROM drive presents a more economical alternative than implementing a network and paying the network license fee.

Applications that comprise several discs can benefit by "daisy-chaining" two or more drives together to search them both at the same time. This eliminates the need for disc swapping and some duplication of effort involved in rekeying search strategies.

Single Workstation, Multiple Products

Another, more common, alternative would run a combination of products on the same hardware configuration. While this solution maximizes the use of limited computer resources, it may require a good deal of disc swapping. This could present logistical problems for storing and managing the discs and security issues that administrators should consider before adopting this approach. We assume that most libraries with limited funds that do not implement a local area network would adopt this solution. Consequently, we shall address in more detail the issues surrounding such a choice.

Assumptions

Each CD-ROM system has a minimum set of hardware and software requirements for proper operation. In addition, vendors usually specify a set of recommended requirements to improve system performance. Potential buyers should familiarize themselves with these requirements before purchasing a given system because this could mean the difference between successful operation and failure.

Hardware

In addition to the microcomputer, a CD-ROM system evidently requires the attachment of a CD-ROM drive which usually comes with an interface card and cable for proper installation. CD-ROM systems once ran exclusively on IBM and compatible computers. However, some clones would not work properly. If you own a clone to which you plan to add a CD-ROM drive, you should verify whether or not it will run on your micro if you have any doubts.

While most products support the major brands of CD-ROM drives, some may work better with one drive than another; or they may not support certain drives. In case of doubt, you should check with the vendor of the CD-ROM drive for hardware compatibility and with the application vendor for product compatibility with the hardware configuration.

With Apple's entry into the CD-ROM market, we see more and more CD-ROMs becoming available for the Macintosh. Some are designed exclusively for that platform. Some operate on both a PC and a Mac. We may see versions developed for other operating systems in the not-too-distant future.

At the 1990 ALA annual conference, Logitech demonstrated its CD Ware system that allows DEC users to access CD-ROM products. Chapter 3 describes this product and other products that extends access to CD-ROM beyond the DOS and Macintosh platforms.

Software

Most CD-ROM products specify a version of the disk operating system (DOS) they require. This is often MS-DOS or PC-DOS 3.1 or higher. Trying to run an application on a lower-numbered version of the software than that specified can result in a system freeze which will require rebooting.

The search and retrieval software and any operating software peculiar to a product usually comes from the vendor of the CD-ROM disc. This could consist of a separate floppy disk or it could reside on the CD-ROM itself.

CD-ROM Extensions

In addition, some programs require Microsoft's MS-DOS Extensions. This is a software program that extends DOS to allow it to overcome the 32-megabyte limitation on file size. It also sets up the CD-ROM drive as an additional drive on the micro. This permits the user to read and access the CD-ROM drive using DOS commands.

This software aims to minimize some of the compatibility problems that existed previously and to make products playable in virtually any CD-ROM drive. However, it does not eliminate the problems entirely.

Some newer products may require a later version of Extensions to work properly. Earlier versions created before the acceptance of the High Sierra standard and, later, the ISO 9660 standard may not work properly with these products.

RAM

While some CD-ROM products may run on as little as 256 or 384K random access memory (RAM), most need 512 or 640K. Many also require the presence of specific peripheral equipment such as a hard disk for storing data files and operating programs, graphics card and monitor, or a mouse. (We assume a hardware configuration with a hard disk.) Purchasers should note any memory requirements as well as any peripherals needed, especially when planning to use the CD-ROM system in conjunction with other software such as word processors and memory-resident programs.

While a particular program may run smoothly in stand-alone mode with the minimum amount of recommended memory, it will need a larger amount if used in conjunction with a word processor. Microsoft's Bookshelf and Bowker's Books in Print Plus represent two such discs that require more RAM memory for use with a word processor.

Computers with more than 640K of RAM may gain some conventional memory (memory below 640K) by running some applications in extended memory (memory above 640K). For example, they can run MS-DOS Extensions from extended memory by loading it with the /E switch to free the conventional memory it would normally use. Chapter 2 discusses the problem of "RAM cram" and possible solutions in more detail.

Memory-Resident Programs

Memory-resident programs come in a variety of forms. Some can be as simple as a program to display the time in the corner of the screen or to sound an alarm at a predetermined time. Others may provide certain functions at the touch of a key. One could have a memory-resident calculator, for example, that will appear on the screen with a single keystroke for use with a word processor or database program. Other, more complicated, programs incorporate several features into a single package for access from within any other program. Examples include products like Deskmate and Sidekick.

The point is that these programs consume memory. They may or may not have a feature to unload them from RAM. This means that they may conflict with some CD-ROM programs that push a system's memory capacity to the limit. This may result in the CD-ROM failing to load properly and exiting to DOS.

More seriously, if the program encounters the problem during operation, it may freeze the system requiring rebooting. Some programs will verify the system configuration before performing certain tasks and return a message that something does not function properly. This avoids freezing the system and gives the operator an opportunity to correct the problem or abort the operation. In our discussion, we assume that all systems meet the recommended hardware and software configuration. We confine ourselves to discussing those products operating within the MS-DOS and PC-DOS environment.

Installation

Virtually all CD-ROM systems come with a program to install the operating software on the local workstation. Sometimes the producer includes it on the CD-ROM disc with the operating software and data files. Often it comes on a separate floppy disk. This disk may include an updated version of the search software. It could also serve to thwart unauthorized access by people who may have an outdated or hand-me-down CD-ROM disc.

Before installing a particular system, users should backup the hard disk or at least the root directory which contains the files that the installation program will modify. Producers usually provide only compiled programs to prevent the user from modifying or tampering with them. Consequently, one cannot read the program to learn what it will do to the files beforehand.

Some installation programs echo to the screen the actions they perform and whether or not they have been successful. Others accomplish their tasks without giving the user any indication of what they did.

A file called INSTALL.BAT or SETUP.BAT often invokes the installation program. Its purpose is to install the search and retrieval or operating software automatically. This should facilitate the user's work. However, it can present some complications if one does not know what is happening because the screen display and the manuals often do not explain what this program does.

AUTOEXEC.BAT File

First of all, the installation software usually creates a subdirectory to group some or all of the programs and possibly some other files such as data files on the working disk--generally the hard disk. It then needs to tell the computer where those files reside and how to access them. To do this, most installation programs modify the AUTOEXEC.BAT file to add these "path" statements that specify file locations and access routes as well as the command to load the product and related software.

This approach assumes that the consumer has a dedicated workstation that runs one and only one CD-ROM product. However, installing multiple CD-ROM products within the same batch file can cause path conflicts. It takes a little programming knowledge and familiarity with constructing batch files to avoid these difficulties.

In addition, upon exiting, some CD-ROM products leave the user in the same subdirectory as the CD-ROM files rather than going back to the root directory. This could result in confusion if one tries to load another program without realizing this fact. The screen will just display the "Bad Command File Not Found" message.

Some producers have recognized this problem. Instead of modifying the AUTOEXEC.BAT file, they now create a separate batch file for their product with all the necessary path statements and file loading commands.

If the INSTALL program does not do this or if you want to protect yourself, you can rename the AUTOEXEC.BAT file prior to installation. After running the program, rename the newly-created AUTOEXEC.BAT file with an appropriate file name and a ".BAT" extension. Then rename the old AUTOEXEC.BAT file to bring it back to its original designation.

This has the effect of minimizing any potential conflicts by creating separate batch files for each application. It also leaves the original AUTOEXEC.BAT intact and lets you select the application rather than have it boot up automatically.

CONFIG.SYS File

The CONFIG.SYS file is another file that installation programs frequently change. This holds especially for proprietary software which does not use Microsoft's MS-DOS Extensions but requires a particular device driver. This file specifies the system configuration. In other words, it tells the computer what peripherals to look for and how much memory to allocate for files and buffers. It governs how the computer works with the various programs.

It also specifies the device driver which is the program that reads, accesses, and controls the operation of the CD-ROM drive. Since the

AUTOEXEC.BAT or other batch file loads the device driver, the driver specified in the CONFIG.SYS and the batch file must agree with each other. Otherwise the system will not be able to read it or function properly.

The CONFIG.SYS file also specifies the drive designation for the CD-ROM drive. This makes the computer aware of the presence of an additional drive and its location. With CD-ROM Extensions and a hard disk drive, the CD-ROM drive will usually have the designation of drive **D**. Large hard disks with two partitions (drives **C** and **D**) will see the CD-ROM drive automatically designated drive **E**. Multiple CD-ROM drives will carry successive letters. Users can also configure their CD-ROM drives to respond to virtually any letter they want such as **L** or **X**.

As the CD-ROM drive should be the last one loaded on the system, most CONFIG.SYS files will include the statement "Lastdrive=Z" (or another letter that designates the position of the last drive).

Files and Buffers

To maximize system efficiency, many CD-ROM products require certain memory configurations. The installation programs check the CONFIG.SYS file for the proper statements and modify them if necessary. This usually involves the number of files and buffers the system accommodates. The number of files indicates the number of files the system can have open at any one time. The number of buffers determines the amount of memory set aside for caching or storing transitory information to avoid repeating time-consuming lookups.

Each file requires an additional 2 bytes of memory. For example, a system which includes a "Files=20" statement sets aside 40 bytes for that purpose. Buffers consume much more memory. Each one sets aside approximately 528 bytes or a little more than 1/2K. Thus, a "Buffers=20" statement reserves 10560 bytes or almost 10 1/2K of RAM. This may seem like a small amount of overhead. However, some products require large amounts of RAM. These necessitate keeping the number of files and buffers to a minimum.

Both the CONFIG.SYS and AUTOEXEC.BAT (as well as all batch files) are written in ASCII (American Standard Code for Information Interchange). This allows the user to read them from

DOS or from a word processor and to modify them, if necessary. Since the system reads the AUTOEXEC.BAT and CONFIG.SYS files only upon booting, any changes to these files requires rebooting for the modifications to take effect.

DOS Patches

A few products--especially proprietary ones--may use patches to DOS to operate. This may involve changing the system's hidden files as occurs in the case of at least one product. These hidden files are the IBMBIO.COM and IBMDOS.COM files which appear as one and two dots at the beginning of a directory listing. These files include the operating programs as well as the input/output programs that govern all the computer's operation.

In addition to being hidden system files, they are also compiled files. This means they appear in machine-readable code, thereby preventing the operator from reading and modifying them. Moreover, the installation program may modify them in such a way that they consume more RAM. Any such modifications will generally produce a conflict when trying to run another CD-ROM product. Changes to the system hidden files are very difficult to identify and correct.

You may not realize this until you try to load a CD-ROM product that requires virtually all of DOS's available RAM and still does not have enough memory. With the acceptance of the ISO 9660 standard, very few CD-ROM applications use DOS patches.

Protecting Yourself

Backup

You can use the Type command to display the contents of the AUTOEXEC.BAT and CONFIG.SYS file to the screen before and after installation to see how they have changed. However, a more useful procedure would involve copying these files to a floppy disk or renaming them to serve as a backup in case of failure or in the event you need to make any modifications.

For this purpose, it would be a good idea to have available somebody such as a system administrator or DOS expert who has some familiarity with DOS and understands the various statements in these files as well as their implications. This person would probably know why the conflict occurred and what to change. He or she could also serve as a resource to resolve any problems or contact the vendor to discuss the problem and work out a solution.

Separate Files

Another alternative would involve creating separate AUTOEXEC and CONFIG files with matching mnemonic extensions. This identifies the two files relating to a particular CD-ROM product. Prior to loading the application, you would copy them into the AUTOEXEC.BAT and CONFIG.SYS files and reboot. Jake Hoffman, in the February, 1988 issue of *CD-ROM Librarian*, (Creating a CD-ROM/PC Reference Workstation pp. 17-20) mentions a program called R.E.Boot that automatically does this.

You can create a batch file to copy the appropriate AUTOEXEC and CONFIG files to configure the system. Including the R.E.Boot program (or one of its relatives such as Warmboot, Coldboot, etc.--all public domain programs available from bulletin boards) automatically restarts the computer and loads the new configuration and device driver files without having to turn off the power or use the CTRL-ALT-DEL key combination.

This option would allow a user to select a program without ever being aware that the system would reinstall configuration and device driver files or restart the computer.

In a follow-up article (CD-ROM/PC Reference Workstation Revisited *CD-ROM Librarian* April, 1989 pp. 9-14), Jake discusses the AUTOEXEC.BAT and CONFIG.SYS files and their intricacies. James Speed Hensinger takes a slightly different approach to the one Jake and I espouse (Using Multiple CD-ROM Databases on One Workstation Or How to Fool the System *Laserdisk Professional* 2:2 March, 1989 pp. 84-87).

Troubleshooting. In the event of a system conflict or problem in loading a particular application, the system manager should check the CONFIG.SYS file to verify that it contains all the necessary statements, the proper device driver, and settings. If this does not solve the problem, you may need to build the AUTOEXEC.BAT file one statement (line) at a time (or related lines together) to verify that each command works properly. You would repeat this process until you identify and correct the problem.

An alternate approach would work backwards, deleting one line at a time until you isolate and correct the problem. The disadvantage of these approaches is that they require frequent rebooting--either hot (using the CTRL-ALT-DEL key combination) or cold (turning off the power for a couple of seconds)--because the computer only reads the AUTOEXEC.BAT and CONFIG.SYS files at boot-up.

Sometimes, the problem could consist merely of a missing space indicator (blank character) which determines whether or not the computer can understand the command which it receives. At other times, it could consist of misplaced or wrong punctuation. A "/" instead of a "\" causes the computer to look for an optional switch to a DOS command rather than for a change in the directory path.

Similarly, one can very easily mistake a ";" (semicolon) for a ":" (colon). The colon should appear after the drive designator when changing drives or to access a program residing on a different drive from the current one. This frequently occurs with setup programs which call the installation program from the CD-ROM disc (D:INSTALL) or a floppy diskette (A:INSTALL) for installation on the hard disk.

Group Applications with Same Device Driver

A third alternative consists in identifying those applications which use the same device driver and system configuration and running them on the same workstation. This would avoid rebooting the system every time someone changes application.

The secret to implementing this alternative effectively in a public service area lies in the ability to create batch files and a menu of all available options with letters or numbers to identify each one. The user merely selects the desired letter or number. Batch files bearing the same names as the letters or numbers listed in the menu can prompt to insert the appropriate CD-ROM disc in the drive, change directory, and load the search and retrieval software. Upon exiting the application, the program should return to the root directory and display the menu again.

Chapter 3 discussed how some applications bypass MS-DOS Extensions and call on the CD-ROM drive directly. These kinds of products may or may not pass control back to the batch file, leaving the user in limbo when exiting a program.

ISO 9660 Standard

Most of the CD-ROM products on the market adhere to the High Sierra or ISO 9660 standards (modified High Sierra). This means that they can all rely on the device drivers that accompany MS-DOS Extensions. Each brand of CD-ROM drive requires its own set of driver commands.

Even the drivers for a particular brand of CD-ROM drive carry different names depending on the source of the software. Some producers still require proprietary device drivers and software which generally come on a separate floppy disk rather than on the CD-ROM. Potential buyers should be aware of this when making purchasing decisions.

Products that adhere to the ISO 9660 standards and use the drivers with MS-DOS Extensions allows compatibility and portability between systems. We can just switch CD-ROM discs and load the appropriate search software without having to reboot the system for every application.

System Management

If a library runs several CD-ROM applications on the same workstation, the system manager needs to be aware of several factors. First, he or she must know the drive designation for the CD-ROM disc. This is particularly important when several drives are daisy-chained together. The drive designation often must appear in path statements to access the data. By switching to the appropriate drive, one can also use DOS commands to display or manipulate files on ISO 9660 standard CD-ROMs.

File Locations

Good file management would put all the necessary files for particular applications in their own directories and subdirectories. We can consider directories like apartment buildings that comprise several apartments (subdirectories). Each apartment has several rooms (files). We can thus consider navigating around directories analogously to moving around an apartment building.

Just as we cannot go directly from the bedroom of one apartment into the next apartment, we need to exit a particular file and possibly change subdirectory to access another file. This indicates the importance of knowing our location on the disk in order to work effectively with the files.

File Clean Up

Installation programs usually create the directory and subdirectory structure; but the system manager should be conscious of this fact and understand the purpose of each file. This knowledge also facilitates navigating around the various applications to work with some of the files. Many applications create work files during operation which should get cleaned up upon exiting. Some products may erase these files. Users may also create files intentionally or unknowingly that remain on the disk. The system manager should examine these directories periodically to clean out these unused files and saved user searches to free up disk space and to improve system performance.

Working with Directories

Most installation programs permit users to rename the directories for the software and operating files. Users should know that the operating programs look for files in these directories. While the installation program should store the new directory names as variables for use within all the programs, there may be some bugs in some programs that continue to search the directories as named by the publisher.

Many applications save user-designated files to these directories for post-processing. Some do not have features to manipulate data directly but let the user save it for later work with word processing or spreadsheet programs. The user needs to know where these files reside in order to access them.

One can type a new path statement at the DOS prompt to tell the computer in which directory to look for files and the order to follow. Otherwise, one would need to use the software's feature to change the logged disk drive or directory to the appropriate path. One might also include the path statement as part of the file name when calling it up.

Instruction

Users may require some form of instruction to search effectively on CD-ROM discs and to navigate around the directories and subdirectories to work with the results of their searches. Some of us may want to provide specific information in a classroom setting in addition to posting searching aids near the workstations. Since most libraries will not have the resources to devote a complete system to educational purposes, many of us may find ourselves moving a workstation from its usual location into the instruction area. This may involve moving the various components piece by piece or all together on a rolling cart.

Although computers are much more durable today than they were a mere decade ago, we must still be careful about how we handle them. Moving them around can cause jolts going over thresholds, bumping walls or furniture, or even dropping them. This can knock the heads out of line and require repair to use the computer again. Many software producers realize that users need to move their computers from time to time. In order to provide a little protection to the heads during this process, many versions of DOS--especially the more recent ones--include a program that effectively "parks" the heads. This involves placing the read/write heads over a location of the disk that does not contain any data. In the event of a jolt, any disk damage should not result in any data loss. Users of earlier versions of DOS can obtain similar programs from public domain and shareware sources. These programs have various names such as SHIP, SHIPTRAK, or PARK.

One just needs to type the appropriate command before turning the power off. The program may display a message indicating what it will do and ask for confirmation. Turning off the power "parks" the heads for transport. Turning the power back on automatically "unparks" them and makes the computer ready for operation.

Tape Loading

Large libraries that have heavy demand on certain databases may wish to get site licenses to the database tapes for loading on a mainframe or minicomputer. This approach would probably result in better performance as the storage medium works faster than the relatively slow CD-ROM drive.

Accessing CD-ROM Drives from a Mainframe or Minicomputer

Another alternative would link a CD-ROM drive to a mainframe or a minicomputer. Because mainframes and minicomputers use different operating systems, this choice will require writing new device drivers to operate with the particular brand of computer. It may even necessitate rewriting the search software to optimize performance.

CD-ROM systems have established themselves as reputable research tools since their introduction in 1985. They have found widespread acceptance in libraries. Although standardization has resulted in greater portability and simpler operation, there still remain a number of possible problems and challenges to consumers who wish to work with more than one application on a single workstation. We addressed some of them in this chapter. The more one knows about how a particular system operates, the easier it will be to make it perform as desired. It will also facilitate troubleshooting and problem resolution.

6
Future Considerations
George A. Sands, Jr.

It seems like only yesterday (actually it was 1986) when we first started plotting our strategies for use of CD-ROMs in our library. What began as a rather straightforward attempt to sample some "new" technology became an often frustrating but frequently rewarding journey into the world of networked CD-ROMs.

Although my staff may, on occasion, wake up screaming in the night from CD-ROM networking nightmares in their past, they are evidently more comfortable with the current network status, since I am still alive to tell this tale. In fact, networking war stories have now replaced cold sweats. A camaraderie has developed since the actual implementation of the network, in early 1987; and the distant memory of those traumatic times has taken on a warm glow...like boot camp!

Back then, we had no one to call about networking CD-ROMs. Vendors concentrated on getting their single use products to market. They looked suspiciously on networking heresy (some still do). Networking experts for both hardware and software remained unsure how or if the hardware/software equations would work. Every step often became a painful process of trial and error. Even today, when vendors tell us that their products will do exactly what we want and work exactly as they describe, the only true test is to try the products as evaluation copies and see for ourselves. Sometimes they work; sometimes they don't.

Now, CD-ROM networks proliferate like lemmings. The basic approaches remain fairly standard. With enough hardware, software, and some technical expertise, a CD-ROM network can become part of the fabric of nearly any organization. In fact, creating and pressing one's own CD-ROM products comes closer to reality as hardware and software continue to appear at lower and lower prices. When will the cost of digitizing data onto CD-ROMs cost less than maintaining that data in paper format? Perhaps it will come sooner than we think.

Yet, despite all the progress made during the past few years, much needs to be done. We must address the concept of remote access, not only from the technical achievement aspects but also from the vendor's standpoint. Prohibiting use of CD-ROM products via telecommunications unfairly restricts library users who will never buy that CD-ROM product. We also need to explore other issues including RAM cram and the means of access (telephone lines, fiber optics, and such).

Connectivity

The issues of connectivity within and among LANs and between LANs and minicomputers or mainframes need further exploration and development. The use of very user-friendly expert systems and hypertext components to facilitate access to data needs considerable improvement.

How nice it would be if CD-ROMs used standardized procedures and protocols for loading and use! Even a software program which could interpret the different protocols of various search engines would help by allowing the user to learn just one program, thus facilitating access to all products.

Along these same lines, how many network managers dread the appearance of the latest and greatest software upgrades for various CD-ROM products that appear from time to time? Often, loading and running these upgrades is fairly easy; and the systems function transparently, as if nothing had happened. Many times, however, the network administrator must make phone calls for technical support and tweak the system to run the upgrade, wasting time and leading to frustration for both patrons and staff.

For larger LANs or those with some heavily used products, networking software that automatically balances loads would be useful. By load balancing, the network administrator could place multiple copies of a heavily-used product on a network. The network, in turn, could read heavy usage and direct users to the least-used copies. This would reduce the likelihood of slowdowns, with too many users trying to gain access to a single CD-ROM.

RAM Cram

RAM cram presents another recurring issue. Loading necessary software (DOS, etc.) on a network, reduces the amount of available RAM to run a specific product's software. If the product requires a lot of memory, the system might not have sufficient RAM to let it operate in the network environment. This presented more of a problem in the past with certain CD-ROM products. Today, it seems less of one, as vendors recognize the concerns, and use software and other tweaks, including expanded memory cards, to circumvent them.

Wouldn't it be nice, though, if CD-ROM vendors would write their software so we could load it into "extended memory" above 640K? This would resolve the RAM cram problem and allow for more memory-intensive software if necessary.

Perhaps most important, we need a greater variety of more useful, user- friendly, full text CD-ROMs. They should have more reasonable prices too. Instead of trying to sell 3000 copies at $3000 each, why not sell 30,000 copies at $300? And from the networking and remote use side, why not just charge the base price or at worst no more than 1 1/2 times the base price? The prevailing paranoia that selling just one copy of a product will let everyone in the world use it just does not hold true.

So, despite the fact that we've come a long way in a short time, we have a long way to go with CD-ROMs both to increase and to maximize their efficient use in library networks. And, as we continue to see, new and grander hardware and software appears before existing issues get resolved.

Yet, who would have thought we would ever use laser printers, scanners, and large storage devices or think about such things as computer-aided software, read/write optical storage in the gigabytes, CD-ROM jukeboxes, and operating systems such as UNIX and OS/2? These products exist today; but their utility and cost must temper their purchase.

Jukeboxes

As a CD-ROM network grows, so does the need for additional CD-ROM drives. This can become troublesome, given the cost of those drives as well as the potential trauma of dealing with a wall of drives and controller cards.

One possible aid, an offshoot of CD audio technology, comes in the form of a CD-ROM jukebox, a product which did not exist when we first implemented our network. Pioneer Electronic Corporation has introduced the DRM-600/DRM-610 CD-ROM MiniChanger and DRM-A600 6-Disc Magazine which can house both CD-ROM and CD audio discs.

The removable magazine can house six CD discs, nearly four gigabytes of data. Users can daisy-chain several of the changers together using a single controller card to give access to a total of 42 CD-ROM discs...wonderful!

Alternate configuration schemes allow a changer to use six different data sources or support a single, multiple-disc data source. The changers support CD-ROMs which conform to the ISO-9660 or High Sierra formats. They have a built-in stereo headphone jack and audio connectors for connection of an external sound system, wonderful for CD audio and those talking, singing, or tweeting CD-ROMs (e.g. Multi-Media Birds of America). With two SCSI ports and a seek time of less than one second, this product may provide some options for those with more CD-ROMs than drives. All this at a price under $1,500.

One caveat: in a jukebox approach, only one person at a time can use only one disc at a time--a real limitation for heavily-used CD-ROMs. For less popular titles, however, a jukebox could house a single product comprising several discs or several different products. Network administrators could incorporate them into a network with other CD-ROM drives or, maybe less problematically, attach them directly to PCs in a work area, with each PC having access to that jukebox. While it has its limitations, it may serve a need in certain circumstances at good price performance.

But CD-ROMs have been around for a while. They're "old" technology. What about the future, the bleeding edge of technology?

Multimedia Computing

Nicholas Negroponte of MIT sees speech-controlled computers; Bela Hatvany of SilverPlatter envisions information malls. Various writers, thinkers, and futurists see the integration of television and computers. The future, according to some of them, lies in the interactive multimedia machine.

Even as I write this, new demons with acronyms like CD-I (Compact Disc--Interactive), DVI (Digital Video Interactive), and CD-ROM XA (CD-ROM Extended Architecture) appear to tantalize and traumatize us. (See the end of the chapter for definitions and explanations of these acronyms.) We should soon see multimedia machines that combine data with graphics, animated graphics, audio, and full-motion video.

We are at the beginning of what promises to be a revolution in information delivery. It will change drastically and forever how and where and what information and the kinds of information we receive. And to stand in the forefront of information delivery (or at least near it) we, in libraries, must redefine our roles or at least adapt to the changes.

Interactive Information

An ongoing argument has ensued over television and the stereo as the last appliances to become an integral part of the American home. Wait a minute, you say. What about the VCR and the CD player? But these are add-ons to the stereo and TV and do not count. Even the personal computer has not yet become pervasive in the vast majority of American homes.

Currently, the television consists of an analog device which allows you to watch a program broadcast to you from a remote location. The viewer has no control over the content or the time of the broadcast. Even as television technology improves (high definition television [HDTV] appears just around the corner), the results will remain the same but with a sharper image.

Picture, if you will, a computer add-on linked to a digital television (a.k.a. computer monitor) all linked by fiber optic cable capable of transmitting multimedia; and the results become mindboggling. The potential of viewer-controlled and manipulated interactive information with hypertext links, sophisticated expert systems, and possibly neural network capabilities would change forever the way we deal with television and information. Do not, however, expect to see all this on the shelves by Christmas! But as research and development on these various processes continues, they should naturally coalesce sometime in the future.

Already, we see changes. As fiber optic networks come on-line and hardware/software costs drop, the demand for long distance multimedia grows. Activities such as video teleconferencing, once the domain of the large corporations, now become affordable for smaller organizations, although not yet for most libraries. Companies even have some low-end desktop conferencing systems in development. As costs continue to fall, libraries may find the resources to take advantage of this technology.

Where corporations target training, project management, and presentations, libraries may also focus, on education, and information transfer. This will move the entire process of networking to a new level of sophistication, efficiency, and user friendliness.

While this sounds pretty exciting, much work lies ahead; and we need to overcome innumerable hurdles. Not in the least, these hurdles include standardized video compression, telecommunications systems which can handle the needed throughput, hardware and software to facilitate the process, and user-friendly applications.

Current networks may operate in the range of two to ten Mbps (megabits per second), for example, Arcnet, Ethernet, with some faster networks (sixteen Mbps Token Ring) now appearing. But the talk in some multimedia circles of a need for transmission rates of 1,000 Mbps to the desktop will not happen in the near future.

However, as I write this, new telecommunications terms and concepts with acronyms like ISDN, SONET, FDDI, and SMDS appear in the press and in the literature. Trying to figure out what they all mean and how they might fit together can be exasperating. Even the experts don't have all the answers.

ISDN

Much recent talk concerns ISDN (Integrated Services Digital Networks) currently under development by regional telephone companies. This first step in the evolution of telecommunications systems offers only a narrowband product with a primary rate of 1.5 Mbps, inadequate for high speed LANs or WANs, high definition video, hypermedia, and the like.

Some have proposed a broadband ISDN standard (B-ISDN) which would feature transmission rates of 150 Mbps. Suddenly, multimedia transmissions would become a distinct possibility. The telephone companies are incorporating the fiber optic capacity into their operations to address this heavier traffic.

SONET

High speed SONET (Synchronous Optical Network) interface standards to the fiber optic network would allow switching equipment compatibility and transmission rates of more than 150 Mbps, enough to handle the requirements of B-ISDN.

We should see agreements soon on the Asynchronous Transfer Mode (ATM), a subset of B-ISDN, which defines the size of information cells that move over a high speed network. Political, economic, and technical issues will affect how this all plays out.

FDDI

Then we have FDDI (Fiber Distributed Data Interface) which supports data transmission rates of 100 Mbps, compared to Ethernet, which handles 10 Mbps. The possibility of consolidating a number of slower LAN architectures under an FDDI network and routing information to appropriate locations or developing a LAN which allows this magnitude of speed without the limiting effects of Arcnet or Ethernet or other LAN cards may radically change the configuration, effectiveness, and speed of future LANS as well as WANs.

FDDI uses a ring-like topology; but it is not compatible with Token Ring. It remains expensive due to high component costs. Experts generally view it as a backbone to link slower networks or to connect high speed PCs.

Even before FDDI becomes a household word, news of FDDI 2 appears, like a bad movie sequel, except in this case its development will support video, voice, and data. It will also provide the basis for a true multimedia network.

SMDS

And if that's not enough, SMDS (Switched Multimegabit Data Service) would link LANs over a public network. This kind of service may soon become available from the telephone companies. It could facilitate remote access among networks in lieu of T1 and T3 lines. This could become the precursor of broadband ISDN, although it has some incompatibilities that could adversely affect a migration path from SMDS to B-ISDN.

Networking Networks

This concept of networking networks may, initially, take the form of a MAN (Metropolitan Area Network). Typically a MAN would connect high speed LANs to backbone wide area networks or WANs. A MAN would feature very high data rates, transmission rates of more than 100 Mbps, coverage over a wide geographical range, a low error rate, and potential connections to numerous stations.

It could also utilize the FDDI standards or another protocol called the IEEE 802.6 standard using the aforementioned SMDS or DQDB (Distributed Queue Dual Bus) which appears to have the support of the telephone companies. The key features of DQDB include its flexibility in dealing with the requirements of handling a diversity of data types and two busses which handle transmissions (sending and receiving) in opposite directions.

Over the next few years, it will be interesting to see how these telecommunications approaches evolve, whether they can integrate with one another, which prevail, and which fail, and what new and better ideas appear. Dramatic changes in telecommunications will have a significant impact on the way we handle information.

Much work lies ahead, however, in the development of standards, experimentation, and design--all of which will have significant impact on the direction, requirements, and specifications of library LANS.

Data Compression

The advent of elaborate multimedia products introduces another important part of the multimedia puzzle--data compression. Multimedia requires tremendous mass storage and realistic data transfer rates. A TV quality display requires a rate of 720 kilobytes per frame displayed at 30 frames per second. This means that one second of video devours 22.1 megabytes of storage. At that rate, a CD-ROM could only store 30 seconds of video. With a transfer rate of 150 kilobytes per second, it would take an unreasonable five seconds to display a single frame.

But the elegant concept of compressing all that data into a smaller size and decompressing it when used needed refinement. More specifically, compression schemes for data, audio, and similar content had existed for some time; but the capability to compress video and decompress it in real-time remained a difficult problem until DVI technology provided a solution.

A few years ago, it did not seem feasible that a PC could perform data compression cheaply; but, as the multimedia game heats up, a variety of compression schemes appear on the scene. Where it all will end is anyone's guess.

Intel Corporation, the leader in DVI technology, offers two ActionMedia products called the 750 Capture Board and the 750 Delivery Board which list for $2,150 and $1,995 respectively. The delivery board allows playback of full motion video, still images, graphics, high quality audio, and all the multimedia goodies on a CD-ROM, hard disk, or other digital random access device via a single board mounted in a PC. The capture board does just that, allowing a PC to capture and digitize video and audio from live or recorded sources. It can be used in conjunction with the delivery board as an authoring platform or in end-user systems.

Discrete Cosine Transform

Now, other compression approaches are appearing. C-Cube Microsystems, Inc. has developed a compression chip based on a standard approved by the Joint Photographic Experts Group, or JPEG, that uses the compression algorithm known as discrete cosine transform (DCT). This algorithm differs fundamentally from that developed for DVI; and it's on a single $150 CL550 chip!

DCT compression theory has developed standards which will address high resolution, real-time video, still image compression, video mail, and conferencing.

And now, just when you thought it was safe to forget about data compression, another approach based on fractal geometry rears its head. Iterated Systems is developing this system which differs from most of those under exploration. Presumably, it can produce forty-five seconds of video from each megabyte of storage. This could mean approximately eight hours of video per CD-ROM or somewhat less with audio.

Here, too, further design and development remains. Will the image quality and color depth suffice? What about the price performance? Will this aproach necessitate a revised standard? What else is under development?

This all sounds exciting, interesting, and premature--and it is. Standards are just developing. No broad based applications exist. Current operating systems may not be able to handle these changes, and the costs may be very high, particularly in the beginning. Network management will, in all likelihood, have to undergo major changes. A myriad of other problems and concerns could slow progress. And, despite all this, it's probably going to happen! So where are we now and how do we get there from here?

Microsoft's Vision

Bill Gates, Chairman of Microsoft, has articulated what he sees as the growth path for multimedia over the next few years. The first stage consists of an 80286 or better PC with 640K of RAM and DOS or Windows, a VGA graphics board and monitor, and CD-ROM XA. The second stage will include Windows, a megabyte or more of memory, CD-ROM XA, enhanced VGA, and audio with a digital signal processor. The third stage will run OS/2 Presentation Manager and will use CD-ROM XA and DVI applications.

Although this perspective represents that of a single corporation intent on selling its product line into the future, Mr. Gates's reasoning may be accurate based on the large installed base of 80286 machines in current use. If this machine actually gets built or if its architecture ultimately becomes 80386-based or whether add-ons to existing machines will fulfill the requirements, it has exciting possibilities.

Microsoft's vision of an 80286 or better multimedia machine would include at least a 10 megahertz clock speed; two megabytes of RAM; a CD-ROM drive with at least a one second seek time; a 30-40 megabyte or better hard disk; VGA color; a digital/analog convertor to handle audio; voice synthesizer; support for CD audio and digital sound; audio mixing; and ports for a mouse, joystick, and musical instrument control network as well as a keyboard.

CD-I

The CD-I concept will make a splash with consumers in early 1991 according to CD-I spokespersons. The CD-I player consists of a self-contained machine with a CD drive built in. It is a computer which uses the Motorola 68000 family of chips and features its own proprietary operating system, CD-RTOS (Compact Disk Real Time Operating System).

According to CD-I spokespersons, CD-I aims at the home market. Targeted for release during the first quarter of 1991, a home CD-I player will retail initially for $995. It will include the CD drive and electronics in a single box. It will have the capacity for an input device such as a mouse or joystick. It can output data to a television and through a stereo system. It will also play audio CDs and maybe CD-ROM XA.

A current, industrial version of the player is designed for developers. This category has three levels of machine:

Level 1. A starter system consisting of a three box player with a CD drive and hard disk drive. This allows emulation of a CD-I product from data stored on the hard disk. It gives the developer the flavor of CD-I; but it lacks a few useful items which appear in the next level.

Level 2. Adds a PC or a MacIntosh computer to capture audio or video.

Level 3. Adds a Sun Systems UNIX-based workstation. Adding video boards can provide full motion video.

Software for capturing data for development of a CD-I product can consist of an off-the-shelf product, such as Pixel Paint for the MacIntosh or similar ones for PCs. Other appropriate off-the-shelf software may serve to capture audio, images, and other formats.

While the developer model players have the capacity to incorporate Ethernet boards, this option primarily aims to assist CD-I product developers to network their efforts. CD-I may have the capability to network text; but a network cannot realize the full advantages of CD-I, according to CD-I spokespersons. Currently CD-I will not function in a PC LAN; but it does support NSF networking protocols.

Capacities

One CD-I disc can contain 650 megabytes of data. That boils down to the equivalent of some 300,000 pages of information--

enough data to fill 1,000 floppy disks, show 7,000 photographic quality pictures, or feature audio in the following configurations: 18 hours, 40 minutes of AM radio quality; 9 hours, 20 minutes of Mid-fi; 4 hours, 40 minutes of Hi-fi; or 1 hour, 10 minutes of CD-audio quality. Product developers can configure any combination of these with a corresponding loss of quantity of data storage in the individual media types.

The new consumer and industrial players will include up to 72 minutes of full motion video capability. It will have better quality than VHS, 260 lines horizontal with 525 scanning lines according to CD-I spokespersons. The chip developed to incorporate full motion video uses the algorithm of the discrete cosine transform method discussed earlier.

Although primarily focussed on the home market, we should continue to watch it. With glitzy, attractively priced software in the works and equipment that can do double duty as a CD audio player and CD-I machine or more with the addition of various device drivers, a heavy consumer market share could necessitate library provision of software and in-house utilization of CD-I. Perhaps some heretofore-unknown method will achieve networkability.

However, if CD-I is marketed and viewed as an add-on TV/stereo appliance, however, it may find limited applicability to the current computer market. A large market share in homes without computers and an evolution to a computer platform could present an interesting development. This would only happen as player prices dropped and more exciting, inexpensive software became available, something akin to the CD audio market.

DVI: Digital Video Interactive

A patron or student walks into the library, sits before a computer screen, touches a button, and interacts with a "live" person who leads him or her through an orientation program, including a video tour featuring a walk-around with 360 degree vistas. The program teaches use of the library and gives the user options to explore. Or a patron who needs literacy training approaches the system in a similar fashion and privately improves reading skills interactively with pictures, audio, and video.

Both scenarios just begin to scratch the surface of the possibilities available with Intel's Digital Video Interactive or DVI technology.

DVI provides digitized, full-motion, full screen video, still images, graphics, text, and stereo audio in an interactive environment right on your personal computer. It allows for the storage and manipulation of these media to maximize ease of use and effectiveness.

Simplifying the way in which people use computers, more in harmony with the way we communicate with each other, visually, aurally, and interactively, will revolutionize computer use among users and non-users alike.

Data Compression

The keys to DVI lie in it's ability to manipulate an exciting array of media from a variety of random access storage devices in real-time and in its data compression schemes.

Currently, Intel chooses CD-ROM as the storage device of choice because it is portable, relatively inexpensive, not constrained by DOS partitions, and holds nearly 650 megabytes of data. Remember when a 20 megabyte hard disk seemed large? CD-ROM's 150 KB/second or 1.2 MB/second configuration offers a perfect match for motion video requirements. These factors currently outweigh the disadvantages of CD-ROM (slower seek times than hard disks, read only capability, etc.).

Maybe when huge hard disk storage devices in the terabytes or compression schemes that really put on the squeeze or even the use of read-write optical disks become a reality, the economies or advantages of other storage devices will prevail. But right now, CD-ROM presents a good choice unless you're loaded with megabytes or megabucks.

Data compression algorithms convert analog video signals to digital form and allow compression and decompression of those signals. This is a vital element in DVI technology, since it circumvents the storage capacity and access rate problems mentioned earlier. Without compression and decompression, a CD-ROM could only store 30 seconds of video and it would take more than an hour to view it.

As I mentioned earlier, other firms have or are developing their own compression schemes. But Intel positions DVI in an interesting way: as a general digital, video signal processor. It will have sufficient flexibility to process different compression algorithms based on whatever standards or schemes appear. It should include standards of JPEG (Joint Photographics Experts Group) for compression of digital photographs, MPEG (Moving Pictures Expert Group) for compression of full screen video, or Px64 which focuses on compression of video for transmission over digital networks, and any other group or process or new standard.

Standards

While I'm talking about standards I should mention the two groups now defining standards: The International Standards Organization (ISO) which oversees JPEG and MPEG and the International Consultative Committee on Telegraph and Telephone (CCITT) which works on Px64, video and audio for video conferencing activities. According to Intel, they plan, over the next two years, to lower prices, improve performance, port to different operating systems (OS/2 and UNIX), and standardize DVI as a feature on PC motherboards (reducing from board to chip or chip set size?) while maintaining backward compatibility to support any DVI product ever created. That coupled with one other factor, software, could bring DVI and multimedia into libraries across the country.

A supply of software--multimedia CD-ROMs, if you will--will probably make DVI a reality for libraries. It will offer libraries new avenues of communication and information to improve performance, enhance information dissemination capabilities, and provide a simpler way of authoring multimedia CD-ROMs to allow development of tailor-made library products. The former will probably have the greatest impact in the near future.

Authoring Multimedia Products

Authoring multimedia CD-ROMs becomes rather complex, and is probably too difficult and cumbersome for most libraries. Intel has developed an Application Development Platform (ADP), a set of hardware and software products for development in the C language. It includes an 80386, 25 MHz, PC with the appropriate add-in boards and authoring software among other components. This allows capture and development of images and video at lower frame speeds (10 frames/sec.) called the ELV or edit video level.

After completing the application, developers can send a tape of it to Intel's Compression Service in Princeton, New Jersey, to convert the application to its final Presentation Level Video (PLV), a higher level of performance, if desired. This comes at a price, however. Intel spokespersons say that current PLV compression prices run about $250 per video minute. Add to that all the requisite costs for production and authoring; and it's obvious that most libraries will want to wait for commercially available products.

Networking DVI

The million dollar question remains whether and how DVI will work in a network environment. In a discussion with Jim Jeffers of ProtoComm, working at the Intel facility in Princeton, we discussed the possibilities.

Earlier, I mentioned that the tranfer rate for full motion video of 150 KB/sec. is the same for CD-ROMs. This makes the shiny disc a good medium for DVI. The complexities and requirements of networking, however, make this less so. Using CD-ROM would allow one stream of full screen, full motion video to be moved over a LAN. And that would use the full capacity of the CD-ROM's transfer rate.

In order to effectively incorporate DVI, a network should have the capacity to deliver more than one stream of video simultaneously. If five simultaneous users wanted video information, a LAN file server would have to access and deliver at that rate. Let's use some rough estimates. An Ethernet LAN operates at 10 Mbps and Token Ring up to 16 Mbps. Error correction, software, and other LAN requirements can take up roughly 50 percent of that capacity. We have left 5-8 Mb for transmission space which may give us the five or so streams we require.

Current networks operate in a fashion which sends data over the lines in bursts or packets of data, a function of the network operating system. Since most networks have mainly shared access to data, this burst approach has worked well, resulting in a satisfactory, reasonable response time.

DVI full motion video requires a continual stream of data. This will require additional software. The ProtoComm people who work on that software project release for the first quarter of 1991, according to Jeffers. The software will allow a LAN file server with standard operating system software and DVI boards to deliver DVI to similarly configured workstations in real-time.

When DVI running on a network becomes available, the storage medium will play an important role. Assuming the LAN's bandwidth can handle the required transmission rates satisfactorily, format will dictate results. A CD-ROM-based DVI product will allow access for only one user at a time on the LAN because one user will need the full transmission capacity of that CD-ROM. Storing the DVI product on a hard disk or a digital medium with similar capabilities may make possible simultaneous multiple use on the LAN contingent upon available bandwidth.

Jeffers thinks we will see larger and larger hard disks or other large storage devices over the years which will facilitate their use with DVI. Compression algorithms, he expects, will not change too dramatically in order to maintain a high quality video image.

He did point out an often overlooked factor. While most discussions center on full screen, full motion video, products that do not require full screen, full motion video may find transfer rates at fewer Mbps satisfactory. While the figures do not correspond in true linear fashion, the use of a quarter screen, full motion video display would reduce the Mbps demands by 75 percent. A variation might involve full screen, lesser quality which would transfer the information but in a somewhat herky-jerky fashion. In any case, these instances will require critical preplanning in the development of DVI software.

Remote access presents another possibility; but, again, this is contingent upon bandwidth considerations. Over the next several years, according to Jeffers, we'll probably see more fairly high speed, but not real-time downloads to LANs. They will, in turn, transmit the information in real-time to their workstations.

Virtual Reality

And finally, for all you cyberpunks, we have artificial reality or virtual reality or even cyberspace, a term coined by William Gibson in his science fiction work, *Neuromancer*. Cyberspace referred to a futuristic computer network which people could use by plugging their brains into it. The synonyms of artificial or virtual reality refer to a computer simulation in which the user interacts in three dimensions. The user wears 3-D goggles and a glove which acts as a hand tracking input device, connected to a computer which creates the sensation of touching or manipulating illusory objects in the computer program.

Before you begin proceedings to have me committed, bear in mind that last Christmas, some 700,000 people purchased Mattel Toys' Power Glove, an artificial reality-like item that translates hand and finger movements into electronic signals which can control Nintendo games.

And artificial reality has even more significant possibilities. NASA has been experimenting with virtual environments of the moon and planets for purposes of exploration. It sees application in telerobotics where robot arms emulate the real thing in hazardous environments.

Some exploratory work involves the areas of surgery simulation, the concept of a virtual desk for a paperless office, a skid simulator for practicing safe driving skills, a remote access system which lets an architect and a client, in different cities, inspect a building before it's built. When you stop to think about it, virtual reality has extraordinary possibilities.

New developments in lightweight, 3-D goggles, magnetic positioning systems, advanced graphics chips, and creative human/computer interfaces have made this possible.

While the concept of virtual travel, which would allow me to go on vacation without leaving my computer screen (I wonder if I can get a virtual tan?) may seem a bit outlandish and may lead to new catch phrases like glove-and-goggle-potato, it could manifest itself in the capability of remotely manipulating the same sensory computer program. This could have serious educational, scientific, and industrial applications.

As parts of the puzzle begin falling into place--more powerful hardware, sophisticated software, advanced telecommunications, multimedia, artificial reality and other as yet unthought of concepts--the entire process of information access and transfer will change radically, as will the role of libraries.

The greatest changes may well come in the networking of networks, thereby broadening our access to a tremendous array of data and providing the means to manipulate and mold that data into a useful form. If we expect to respond to our patrons' demands, we must prepare to use these emerging technologies to provide the information they need now and in the future.

Definitions

Now a few definitions are in order for acronyms I used earlier:

CD-ROM XA (Compact Disc Read Only Memory Extended Architecture). Developed jointly by Philips, Sony, and Microsoft, this multimedia format is an extension of the CD-ROM standard. It allows the simultaneous playback of text, graphics, still-image video with low to medium grade audio. It operates through a standard PC with a VGA monitor. Although one can use it with a standard CD-ROM drive, it requires a special "XA" controller card.

CD-I (Compact Disc Interactive). This allows incorporating on one disc data, audio, still video, animated graphics, and partial screen full motion video. Software will feature interactive games, educational, and other databases. Developed by Sony and Philips, it requires a CD-I player. Although industrial-level machines exist, proponents see it as a consumer product for connecting to a television or PC. CD-I discs will not play on a standard CD-ROM drive; but CD audio discs will play on CD-I players. CD-ROM XA *may* operate on CD-I players but only after XA standards are finalized. We should note that, upon release of the consumer model player, we can anticipate the inclusion of a video chip allowing the use of full screen, full motion video.

DVI (Digital Video Interactive). Originally developed by RCA engineers but acquired by Intel in 1988, DVI includes data, audio, graphics, images, and full motion video. It uses a standard CD-ROM player or other random access storage device but requires a DVI controller card in a PC. It allows a user to control the display and manipulate the image. Both Intel and IBM back the DVI approach.

7
LANs, Licenses and Copyright
Meta Nissley

As technology progresses, enabling simultaneous and multiple-use access to information products and services, CD-ROM local area networks (LANs) are becoming a reality rather than a concept in today's libraries. By and large, those involved in setting up local area networks in libraries may tend to focus on resolving the immediate technical challenges inherent in networking systems. Finding sources of funding, solving hardware and software compatibility problems, and managing the networking environment constitute primary concerns that librarians and other information specialists must resolve.

Less immediate than trying to get the network up and running, perhaps, is looking at what comes with the product in the form of a licensing agreement. Librarians should devote attention to investigating copyright protection and to the lease or licensing agreements for individual CD-ROM products which they desire to network. Each individual CD-ROM product may have its own licensing agreement which will govern how buyers may use that product, and whether or not they may put it on a network.

Lease or Licensing Agreements

Lease or licensing agreements are very specific, stating the terms and conditions of each product's use. Generally, the publisher, who may sometimes be the information provider, that is, the holder of copyright for the intellectual property which has resulted in a particular product, handles them. H. W. Wilson, for example, is both the publisher and information provider or copyright holder for its products. Except for the few "families" of products obtainable from an individual electronic publisher, which have similar protective agreements, or the few publishers and/or information providers who do not have licensing agreements, each product requires review of the respective licensing agreements by a librarian or other information specialist. The librarian may then wish to negotiate with the publishers about multiple and/or simultaneous use and price for a particular product on a local network, depending upon the content of the written agreement. Reviewing agreements can become a time-consuming process, particularly if it requires direct negotiations between the librarian and the publisher and/or information provider.

In turn, publishers who are not the information providers or copyright holders must negotiate terms and conditions for the use and dissemination of that intellectual property. Take SilverPlatter as an example; the company may provide software and marketing for a specific product, but it may not actually own the information. SilverPlatter must negotiate with the information provider, such as the American Psychological Association or JA Micropublishing, Inc., for instance, meaning that for each association or company a separate agreement may, in fact, be reached.

This accounts for the differences in licensing agreements for products, even when distributed by the same information provider or publisher. This is magnified in networking environments which may consist of several products, each from different publishers, so that buyers must examine each licensing agreement individually, and any negotiations which may take place occur separately. It also means that publishers should connect with each other regarding each others' software and licensing agreements if they support networking situations.

Control of Intellectual Property

Apprehension about loss of control over the dissemination of intellectual property, in an era of facile electronic duplication constitutes the driving force behind restrictive agreements by copyright holders and information providers. Librarians, lawyers, information specialists, publishers, and information providers all endeavor to come up with equitable solutions and answers to the issues of "fair use" and "fair compensation" for new technologies from each one's perspective. Although publishers of electronic databases, librarians, and copyright holders have not come to complete agreement, the market drives practice and policy to the extent that each party must make compromises to market products. Librarians must be willing to compensate publishers and copyright holders for their intellectual and financial investments for products which libraries demand. The state-of-the-art in compact disc technology is such that duplication of a product to another disc in libraries is not yet a problem. However, limiting access to databases where the potential exists for wholesale downloading and manipulation of data seems to be the focus of the problem with CD-ROM technology.

Copyright History

The original Copyright Act of 1909 intends to promote the distribution of useful scientific information to the public for the benefit of society. Although it protected the intellectual property rights of authors, it was conceived with the idea of making information available. At the time this was being written, copyright law specifically spoke to the protection primarily of literary property and musical works. Since that time, authors and publishers have continually pointed out that the Copyright Law (Title 17 of the U. S. Code) needed amendments to provide better protection for different forms of intellectual property, such as works of art, sound recordings, etc. To address problems encountered with the original 1909 Act and to accommodate various forms of media in addition to written works, Congress revised the law under the Copyright Revision Act of 1976. It specifically addressed the newer technologies of photocopying, public broadcasting, and cable television (CATV).

Fair Use

Although the new act provides broader protection and allows for the principle of "fair use," the law is still far from perfect in addressing today's needs. In an electronic age, with new technologies, new modes of access, and new terminology appearing frequently, traditional copyright protection faces challenges. For instance, protection of software programs has become more complicated than with other more traditional literary works because of the ease of reproducing and disseminating software. Additionally, software, as a product, may enjoy protection not only by copyright law. Patents and trade secret laws, depending on the interpretation of the actual work involved by individuals in the creation or production of the work, could also protect software. For some formats, in this case software, copyright law has proven fairly ineffective for outright protection of the works of authors. Copyright law in itself falls short of accomplishing what it was designed for with respect to the dissemination or protection of intellectual property using new technologies, leaving interpretation of the law to be settled in the courtroom on a case-by-case basis.

No doubt, "fair use" is a phrase familiar to most librarians. Many of us have committed library staff hours to tracking interlibrary loan use, worked with faculty to determine what they can use in the classroom and the length of time they may keep it, warned the public about copyright infringement as posted on copy machines, and negotiated with publishers to obtain copy permission for exceptions to their copyrighted works.

However, when the question of "fair use" is raised with electronic media, a haze begins to descend. What constitutes the parameters for "fair use" when applied to electronic formats? One would invoke the same criteria as for other media, such as the amount and substantiality of the portion used, the nature of the copyrighted work, the purpose of the use, whether it was for nonprofit educational purposes or commerical ones, and the effect on the potential market of the copyrighted work. One should take all of the above into consideration.

It is still difficult, though, to paint a clear picture of exactly what constitutes fair use. For instance, would it be considered "fair use" for an individual to download thousands of records from a bibliographic database found on a CD-ROM, to manipulate those records to his satisfaction, and then, perhaps, to prepare a document or software product for possible commercial purposes? In this scenario it seems clear that most of us would agree that this example would not fall into the category of fair use. However, would it be considered fair use if an individual downloaded the same number of records for purposes of research? Should there be a limit to the number of records which can be downloaded? When it comes to defining what constitutes "fair?", I suspect there is still a lack of consensus among those in the information industry, particularly when we ask, "fair to whom?" It is much more difficult to define in a broad sense than on a case-by-case basis.

Lease and Licensing Agreements

Copyright holders, responding to the ambiguity of the copyright law, have sought stronger protection for their intellectual property. Their efforts to seek stronger protection resulted in lease or licensing agreements. Agreements, in a sense, "overprotect" a product. A consumer, for instance a library, must agree to comply by signature with the terms and conditions as listed on the agreement before purchasing, leasing, or using the product. Although some lease/licensing agreements, such as "shrink wrap" licenses, have not proven successful in protecting rights in court, they have been, nevertheless, consistently used in the industry in addition to copyright protection.

The popularity of licensing agreements rose with the widespread dissemination of software packages. There are few software and optical disk products which do not have licensing agreements today. Publishers and copyright holders tend to opt for a licensing agreement as further protection for their intellectual property. A minority of publishers exist who choose not to require licensing agreements, for example, H. W. Wilson.

Pricing

The price of a product constitutes one element of the value of information. There are varieties of combinations of pricing schemes from different publishers regarding terms and conditions for use, downloading and networking restrictions and disposition of archival copies for CD-ROM products. Until recently, most publishers restricted use of CD-ROM products to a single station and a single user at a time. Due to consumer interest and demand for networking environments, however, publishers need to reconsider their policies about single use, multiple use, and remote access. *PC Magazine* mentions, "Even those few companies that believe networking their databases is a good idea are in a quandary as to how to price and license the multiuser versions." [1]

The most common current policy for publishers who have policies, seems to result in a charge for the basic product and additional fees for additional access. The method of establishing a fee structure for multiuse varies from publisher to publisher. For example, one may charge a flat fee for a multiuser license (e.g. at this writing, PsycLIT charges $5,995 for a multiuser license up to eight stations,

$3995 for a single user). One may charge per additional node while another may charge using a potential use structure (e.g. 1-499 users; 500-1000, etc.). Or, a "pay as you go" model which automatically monitors actual usage. Another may charge by the numbers of enrolled potential users at a particular institution (e.g. 14,000 students).

DIALOG has an interesting matrix system for pricing simultaneous access. DIALOG divides usage into four levels: 2-10 stations, 11-25, 26-60, and over 60. In addition, it has separate price categories for public (e.g. ERIC, MEDLINE) and private sector databases. The customer pays according to the number of stations desired and the sector into which the product falls, in increments of 50 percent for public and 100 percent for private. For specific networking environments over 60, DIALOG will customize systems and negotiate pricing, considering usage patterns, existing hardware and software configurations and design necessary for compatibility and the customer's ability to pay. This model was developed using the PC software industry as an example. DIALOG reports that the bulk of multiuser access stations, so far, falls in the first range (2-10) and that customers have shown a positive reaction to this policy.

Some publishers or information providers, such as H. W. Wilson and EBSCO, do not charge for additional multiuser access (as long as only one player contains the disc), while others still remain in the thinking stages for multiuser license fees and list their policy as, "to be announced" in product price catalogs. At this stage, I believe, librarians have considerable ability to negotiate for individual cases and to adjust pricing structures. Telephone calls to publishers and vendors frequently reveal recent changes in policies and prices. Because networking remains an unknown quantity in terms of what the market will bear, publishers and information providers grope for a reasonable price structure which will allow them to recover their costs and continue product development while establishing reasonable networking price structures for the library marketplace.

The European Association of Information Services (EUSIDIC) has drafted a set of reasonable guidelines for CD-ROM producers. Under "Pricing Principles," it recommends "that prices be simple and clear; it is not considered reasonable to make additional charges for a product used one user at a time even if used in a network environment; and metering or charging for data accessed may be a barrier to full use of the information by the customer." [2]

Remote Dial-In Access

The definition of the term "site," with reference to licensing, varies depending on circumstances and interpretation by the information provider and publisher. In general, a site license is one which has been granted to a specific user at a specific location (i.e. one building). With networking, however, the term may seem broader, yet less tangible. When publishers list the term in a licensing agreement with a library, they do not always specify exactly what a site encompasses. It could constitute a specific location within the library, the entire library, or it could include access from outside the library (i.e. branch libraries). When discussion moves to remote dial-in access from outside one site, some publishers feel real anxiety.

The major contemporary issue pending in this industry is that of remote or dial-in access to databases via a modem. Very few publishers or information providers have a policy in place which addresses the specific issue of networking CD-ROMs and remote access. Among those few who do have policies, several philosophies emerge. For instance, some copyright holders will allow no remote access at all; another will permit remote only after hours (one network license per school); and another will negotiate a multi-site license. It is also likely that any policies which exist today for remote dial-in are "soft" and possibly open to negotiation. Competition among publishers also comes into play when the idea is to have products leased or purchased for use by the public. If companies have no flexibility or interest in satisifying consumers, they lose a potential market, even if the gain results in lower profits than originally expected. The marketplace will, eventually, influence company policy.

Loss of Potential Sales

The apparent apprehension on the part of publishers and information providers comes from the notion that they would lose revenue from potential sales. For instance, a scenario could see one institution purchase a site license, network the CD-ROM product, and allow remote access by those outside the original institution holding the site license, thereby causing the publisher loss of additional sales. For example, a university library might purchase a product for a net-working environment, allow not only its students and faculty access, but also the community at large, including, perhaps, the local public library. Is this a realistic and well-founded concern on the part of publishers and information providers? Is it worth the loss of a sale to the university library?

There are at least two ways of looking at this issue, the legal and the technical. There is obviously a difference in what we would like to be able to do and what is technologically possible. There may be a misunderstanding about how real and widespread remote access networking environments are and would actually become. The present day local area networking systems are designed for use with PCs. Some of the technical problems confronting prospective use of databases via remote control have, as yet, to be resolved. For instance, experts speculate that the overall performance of a network would drop with wide use. Currently, the prevailing opinion among those in the information industry seems to focus on response time which remains slow with remote access stations. However, some think that response time has not constituted as much of a problem as expected since users typically do not conduct exactly the same search simultaneously on the same product.

Costs of Networking

Another consideration focuses on the cost of networking and providing networking services; for instance, dedicated lines and investment in equipment. If publishers must link together various hardware and software product configurations for individual cases, how much would librarians be willing to invest and would it actually provide a service that is cost effective as well as beneficial enough to the community to justify its cost? Justifications for linking CD-ROM products on networks boiled down to saving money overall by reducing the number of stand-alone single workstations, to saving the costs of several individual subscriptions, or compensating for the price of tapeloads or online access. If a network is not cost-effective, what are other intrinsic values and considerations for its development and maintenance? Some librarians may feel outrage at the prices asked by publishers for the capability of multiuser access and networking capability.

Librarians and Copyright Infringement

Librarians have generally complied with copyright restrictions by posting visible warnings to library users about copyright infringement. Copy machines bear warnings about copying printed materials; journal articles obtained through interlibrary loan get stamped with a copyright notice, software programs and videotapes usually carry their own copyright warnings in addition to the library either posting a notice or requiring written acknowledgement of having read such.

Since the 1976 Copyright Revision Act, librarians have taken more active steps to ensure that library users are warned about copyright, infringement, and fair use. It is a responsibility which comes with the profession. That is, to educate library users about their own personal responsibility to respect copyright and to attempt to be fair to authors and publishers who receive fewer royalties and sales when the material is found in a library. However, because of the nature of libraries, whose mission is essentially one of education, which demands the dissemination of information to as wide a community as possible, there is occasional discordance among authors, publishers, and librarians.

When libraries dealt primarily with print works, few restrictive agreements ever appeared from publishers. However, as newer technologies appeared, so did licensing agreements. Rather than seeing fewer agreements, we see more and more. With lease or licensing agreements, basically the same is true as mentioned above. Librarians should adhere to and inform the public about additional restrictions placed on the material as noted on the agreement when purchased or leased. This adds a burden of responsibility of enforcement on the librarian which, in this author's opinion, is unfortunate. It places the librarian in an antithetical role of watchdog in the distribution of information.

On the one hand, publishers typically do not expect each consumer to purchase a set of encyclopedias; but on the other, they do not expect library users to copy each volume from cover to cover. There has been an unwritten but basic policy of self-policing when it comes to monitoring copying in libraries. With newer technologies, the role of the librarian should be to educate the public about its responsibilities regarding copyright infringement. But, as with print products, the process itself should also be self-policing, and the librarian should not have to enforce the law.

The consequences of noncompliance with copyright or licensing restrictions for librarians remain somewhat obscure. We currently have no precedent for violation of a CD-ROM licensing agreement. Although a librarian or other information specialist, even when employed by a state institution, may be personally liable for copyright infringement for materials housed in the library, it is not very likely to happen.

Sovereign Immunity

The Eleventh Amendment to the Constitution has contributed to the difficulty copyright holders face when confronted with infringements by any state and/or individuals employed by state agencies or organizations because of the protection afforded to states through sovereign immunity. Authors and publishers have been able to sue individuals, whether or not they are employed by state agencies (by the way, other governmental agencies are excluded), in cases of alleged copyright infringement. There have been several precedent-- setting cases, particularly with software, which have influenced the degree to which copyright holders and persons employed by state institutions are protected.[3]

In 1989, the Copyright Remedy Clarification Act (H.R.3045) was introduced, passed in the House of Representatives and, to this date, is still pending in the Senate. This bill aims to amend Title 17 to declare that in the future, states will not be immune from suit for violation of exclusive rights of copyright owners. If a change in the law occurs, it may mean, from a layperson's point of view, that although individuals may be less likely to be sued for infringement of copyright protection because of the larger fish (state institutions) to fry, it could also mean that enforcement of copyright protection may increase the numbers of suits against state institutions. This, in turn, could mean less flexibility in the future from libraries and other state agencies in purchasing/leasing new technologies which require licensing agreements with restrictive conditions.

The CD-ROM LAN market remains a relatively new one, and some of the issues discussed here may resolve themselves as more information is forthcoming about technological advances, desirability, and cost, and as we acquire practical experience with them in a networked environment. The construction of reasonable (clear and easy to understand) licensing agreements, should present a goal for publishers and information providers. Librarians, on the other hand, must still take the responsibility of enforcing copyright and licensing agreements where necessary. Again, according to *PC Magazine*, the bottom line is, "You can't assume that there's a legal way to provide multiuser access to a database published on CD-ROM. It's logical, and it's technically possible, but that doesn't necessarily make it legal." [4]

Notes

1. M. Keith Thompson and Kimberly Maxwell, "Networking CD-ROMs," *PC Magazine*, v.9, no.4 (February 27, 1990): 238.

2. "EUSIDIC. Guideline on CD-ROMs: supply conditions and pricing," *The Circular: an OPA publication*, vol. 1, no.3 (October 1989): 3.

3. For more complete information and citations to cases, *see* L. Dobb, "Recent Developments in Copyright Law for New Technologies." In *CD-ROM Licensing and Copyright Issues for Libraries*. Westport, CT: Meckler, 1990.

4. Thompson and Maxwell, 238.

Bibliography

The literature on local area networks is quite extensive. Most of it goes beyond the scope of this work. In fact most local area networks do not support CD-ROM. This bibliography focuses on the literature that pertains more specifically to CD-ROM and to the network operating systems that support it. It includes reviews and evaluative articles about the various software products and the hardware needed to support them as well as buyer's guides.

Akeroyd, J. CD-ROM as an online public access catalogue. *Electronic Library* 6:2 (April, 1988): 120-124.

Bailey, Charles W., Jr. and Kathleen Gunning. The Intelligent Reference Information System. *CD-ROM Librarian* 5:8 (September, 1990): 10-19.

Bass, Brad. USGS converts paper maps to digital images; CD-ROMs, networks improve access and allow customization. (U.S. Geological Survey). *Government Computer News* 8:14 (July 10, 1989): 66-68.

Blacher, Robert. LANtastic offers high performance at bargain prices This peer-to-peer network is easy to use and offers good performance for less than $300 per node. *LAN Technology* 5:5 (May 1, 1989): 54-59.

Bobker, Stephen. One if by LAN. *MacUser* 4:9 (September, 1988): 47-50.

Bridges, Linda and Barry Gerber. Networked CD ROM brings host of advantages. (buyers guide). *PC Week* 6:3 (January 22 1990): 93.

Brunell, D. A LANtastic connection for CD-ROM systems. *OCLC Micro* 6:1 (February, 1990): 12ss.

Buckler, Grant. Bringing power to the people: on-line information no longer the domain of librarians alone. *Computing Canada* 15:17: 20-21.

Buerger, David. CD ROM servers capitalize in LAN connectivity potential. *InfoWorld* 11:43 (October 23, 1989): 41.

Butcher, S. The rewards and trials of networking (CD-ROM databases). *Database* 13:4 (August, 1990): 103-5.

Carey, J. and V. Massey-Burzio. Installing a compact disk network. *College & Research Libraries News* 50:11 (December, 1989): 988-991.

CD-ROM software for networks. (Online Computer Systems' CD-ROM networking software for Novell IPX/SPX and Unix Network File System networks). *The Seybold Report on Desktop Publishing* 4:5 (January 15, 1990): 34-35.

Chandler, Doug. Fresh approaches to CD ROM will spur new growth. *PC Week* 6:3 (January 22, 1990): 91-92.

Chandler, Doug. Software broadens access to CD ROM. (Software Review) (evaluations of three CD ROM networking software packages)(includes related article on testing methods and issues). *PC Week* 6:1 (January 8, 1990): 23-27.

Chen, Ching-chih. Libraries in the information age: Where are the microcomputer and laser optical disc technologies taking us? *Microcomputers for Information Management* 3:4 (December, 1986): 253-265.

Claiborne, David. CD ROM players bring the data to the people. *PC Week* 7:38 (September 24, 1990): 132.

Clegg, Peter. LANtastic. (Software Review) (one of five evaluations of small local area networks). *LAN Times* 7:8 (July, 1990): 128-29.

Derfler, Frank J. LANtastic Network Operating System. *PC Magazine* 7:11 (June 14, 1988): 135, 144.

---------- and Paul Ferrill. LANtastic. *PC Magazine* 8:6 (March 28, 1989): 108, 111.

---------- Low-Cost LANs: Your networking plans don't necessarily have to include high-priced equipment and dedicated servers. Here's a look at 11 systems... *PC Magazine* 8:6 (March 28, 1989): 94-131.

---------- Making do with DOS. (Software Review) (overview of eight evaluations of peer-to-peer networking software)(includes related articles on non-standard products, Server Message Block). *PC Magazine* 9:10 (May 29, 1990): 153-167.

Dryden, Patrick. Meridian boosts LAN CD ROM access speed. *InfoWorld* 12:29 (July 16, 1990): 32.

---------- Opti-Net CD ROM network software adds native Netware support. *InfoWorld* 12:3 (January 15, 1990): 36.

Elshami, Ahmed M. *CD-ROM Technology for Information Managers.* Chicago: American Library Association, 1990.

Folmsbee, Mark Alan, Randall M. Manion, and James M. Murray. Developing Inexpensive MultiUser Access to CD-ROM: LaserCat at Gonzaga University Law School Library. *CD-ROM Professional* 3:3 (May, 1990): 34-38.

Forbes, Jim and Jimmy Guterman. Apple readies CD ROM, AppleShare. *PC Week* 5:8 (February 23, 1988): 3.

Forbes, Jim. Upgraded version of AppleShare LAN to offer CD ROM. (product announcement). *PC Week* 5:9 (March 1, 1988): 6.

Frentzen, Jeffrey. Networking CD ROM meets multiuser storage needs. (buyers guide). *PC Week* 6:12 (March 27, 1989): 132.

Gerber, Barry. CBIS Inc. Network-OS 6.3B. (Software Review) (one of three evaluations of distributed networking software in 'Peer-to-peer nets make sharing easy.'). *PC Week* 7:6 (February 12, 1990): 84-85.

Gerber, Barry and Michael Zimmerman. CBIS Inc. (CD Connection for CBIS Network-OS 1.20A) (Software Review) (one of three evaluations in 'Software broadens access to CD ROM'). *PC Week* 6:1 (January 8, 1990): 28-29.

---------- Artisoft Inc.: LANtastic 2.57g., $495 per network. (Software Review) (one of three evaluations in 'Software broadens access to CD ROM'). *PC Week* 7:6 (February 12, 1990): 84.

---------- LANs and CD-ROM: The quest for a sane, elegant solution. (Net Assets; local area networks; two alternatives for networking CD ROMs) (column). *PC Week* 6:35 (September 4, 1989): 48.

---------- PC networks and CD-ROM: a shotgun marriage at best. (Net Assets). *PC Week* 6:34 (August 28, 1989): 58.

---------- and Doug Chandler. Software broadens access to CD-ROM. *PC Week* 6:1 (January 8, 1990): 23-32.

Gielda, Scott A. Multi-User CD-ROM Systems for Schools and Libraries. *Laserdisk Professional* 2:4 (July 1989): 14-17.

Grant, Marilyn A. and John C. Stalker. The MultiPlatter CD-ROM Network at Boston College. *Laserdisk Professional* 2:5 (September, 1989): 13-18.

Guterman, Jimmy. Network optical drive could address users' gripes about CD-ROM. (product announcement). *PC Week* 5:9 (March 1, 1988): 14.

Halperin, M. and Renfro: Online vs. CD-ROM vs. onsite. High volume searching--considering the alternatives. *Online* 12:6 (November, 1988): 36-42.

Harney, John M. A Comparison of Different CD-ROM Local Area Networks in Universities. *CD-ROM EndUser* 1:2 (June, 1989): 17-22.

Helliwell, John. CD-ROM technology, PC networks still courting stage. (connectivity section). *PC Week* 4:11 (March 17, 1987): C4 ss.

Hewlett-Packard introduces networking capability. *Information Today* 6:8 (September 1, 1989): 20.

Intner, Sheila. *Microcomputer environment: management issues.* Phoenix, AZ. Oryx Press, 1987.

Jones, Del. Advances in massive storage mean increased benefits for local networks. (local area network storage capacity increases promised by new data storage technologies; connectivity section) (column). *PC Week* 4:39 (September 29, 1987): C29.

Kesselman, M.A. Online update [CD-ROM networks]. *Wilson Library Bulletin* 64:5 (January, 1990): 83-84.

Kittle, Paul. Putting a Medical Library Online: Phase III--Remote Access to CD-ROMs. *Laserdisk Professional* 2:3 (May, 1989): 15-18.

Lauriston, Robert. Lantastic 2.53. *PC World* 7:11 (November 1, 1989): 163, 167.

---------- Peer-to-peer LAN serves up additional options Artisoft Lantastic Ethernet, 2-mbps Adapter, 0.7 mbps Adapter, Z. *PC World* 8:3 (March 1, 1990): 96.

Lazzaro, Joseph. Networking with optical disk technology. *LAN Technology* 6:4 (April, 1990): 43-48.

Leggott, Mark. LANs and CD-ROMs. *OCLC Micro* 5:4 (August 1, 1989): 18-22.

---------- CD-ROM and LAN: Some Practical Considerations. *CD-ROM EndUser* 1:3 (July, 1989): 26-28.

---------- and Stephen Sloan. Using CD-ROMs Across a Network: The UNB Experiment. *Laserdisk Professional* 3:2 (March, 1990): 91-93.

Lewis, Linda J. CD-ROM Network in the Classroom. *CD-ROM EndUser* 2:5 (September, 1990): 30-31.

Lynch, Clifford A. and John C. Gale. Multimedia, CD-ROM, and local area networks. *Information Today* 6:8 (September 1, 1989): 19-22.

Maaloe, J. and E. Hornung. Industrial application of optical LAN. Proceedings of the papers presented at the eighth international fibre optic communications and local area networks exposition, 17-21 Sept. 1984, Las Vegas NV. *Information Gatekeepers* 13 (1984): 357-358.

McCormick, John. CD-ROM systems: new hardware expands uses for disk's vast storage. (Government Buyer's Guide). *Government Computer News* 9:9 (April 30, 1990): 52ss.

McGovern, Patricia A. LANLink 5X. (Software Review) (one of five evaluations of inexpensive network software in 'Building workgroup solutions: zero-slot LANs'). *PC Magazine* 9:8 (April 24, 1990): 202-203.

---------- LANtastic/Z. (Software Review) (one of five evaluations of inexpensive network software in 'Building workgroup solutions: zero-slot LANs'). *PC Magazine* 9:8 (April 24, 1990): 204-207.

---------- Printer LAN. (Software Review) (one of five evaluations of inexpensive network software in 'Building workgroup solutions: zero-slot LANs'). *PC Magazine* 9:8 (April 24, 1990): 217-220.

McQueen, Howard. Accessing Databases (LAN Network) (column). *CD-ROM EndUser* 2:5 (September, 1990): 54-55.

---------- Considering a CD-ROM Network? (LAN Network) (column). *CD-ROM EndUser* 1:12 (April, 1990): 61-63.

---------- Minimizing Ongoing Operating Costs (LAN Network) (column). *CD-ROM EndUser* 2:2 (June, 1990): 34-36.

---------- Networking CD-ROMs (LAN Network)(column). *CD-ROM EndUser* 1:11 (March, 1990): 92-95.

---------- Networking CD-ROMs: Implementation Considerations.(LAN Network)(column). *Laserdisk Professional* 3:2 (March, 1990): 13-16.

---------- Remote Dial-In Patron Access to CD-ROM LANs. (LAN Network)(column). *CD-ROM Professional* 3:4 (July, 1990): 20-23.

Madron, Thomas. *Local Area Networks: The Next Generation.* 2nd ed. New York: John Wiley, 1990.

Malloy, Rich. Artisoft speeds up LANtastic. *Byte* 15:2 (February 1, 1990): 84-86.

Manes, Stephen. Standards for CD-ROM software (column). *PC Magazine* 9:3 (February 13, 1990): 91-2.

Marshak, David S. CD-ROM: Listen to the music. (contains related article entitled 'A CD Primer'). *Patricia Seybold's Office Computing Report* 11:4 (April, 1988): 21ss.

Massey-Burzio, Virginia. The MultiPlatter Experience at Brandeis University. *CD-ROM Professional* 3:3 (May, 1990): 22-26.

Maxwell, Kimberly and Patricia A. McGovern. Building workgroup solutions: zero-slot LANs. (Software Review) (overview of five evaluations of serial and parallel connectivity software) (includes related article on Editor's Choices). *PC Magazine* 9:8 (April 24 1990): 187ss.

Maxwell, Kimberly. LANtastic. (Software Review) (one of eight evaluations of peer to peer LAN software in 'Making do with DOS.'). *PC Magazine* 9:10 (May 29 1990): 168-169.

---------- LANtastic Artisoft Inc. *PC Magazine* 9:13 (July 1, 1990): 314-321.

Mayfield, Bruce. Network-OS. *PC Magazine* 9:10 (May 29, 1990): 172, 174.

Mehling, Herman. Meridian setting standards; key catalyst: CD Publisher breaks ice. *Computer Reseller News* No. 342 (November 20, 1989): 109-111.

Mendrinos, Roxanne Baxter. CD-ROM: Research strategies for a lifetime. *Media & Methods* 23:4 (March/April, 1987): 8-11.

Meridian Data offers CD Net. *Information Today* 5:9 (October 1, 1988): 14.

Morrissey, Jane. CBIS to offer Macintosh, CD-ROM links. (product announcement). *PC Week* 5:48 (November 28, 1988): 23.

---------- Low-end Network-OS expands user support. (CBIS Inc.'s Network-OS local area network operating system). *PC Week* 6:42 (October 23, 1989): 66.

Morrow, Blaine V. Do-It-Yourself CD-ROM LANs: A Comparison of LANtastic and CD-Connection. *CD-ROM Librarian* 5:10 (November, 1990): 12-24.

Muchmore, Michael W. New on the market. (First Looks). *PC Magazine* 7:14 (August, 1988): 51-2.

Musich, Paula. New DEC options recast VAX models as LAN servers. (local area networks). *PC Week* 7:28 (July 16, 1990): 37.

Nelson, Nancy Melin. On the cutting edge: Next Technology's CD-ROM jukebox. *CD-ROM Librarian* 4:9 (October, 1989): 22-24.

Nickerson, Gord. Remote Access to CD-ROM. *CD-ROM EndUser* 1:2 (June, 1989): 23,46.

Nissley, Meta and Nancy Melin Nelson. *CD-ROM Licensing and Copyright Issues for Libraries.* Westport, CT: Meckler, 1990.

Olsen, Florence. CD-ROM database service now runs on LANs. (local area networks)(Information Handling Services' Personnel). *Government Computer News* 8:20 (October 2, 1989): 28.

---------- Mingling CD-ROM and LANs: tricky but worth it. (local area network). *Government Computer News* 8:16 (August 7, 1989): 28.

Pemberton, Adam C. LP Interviews Chris Pooley of SilverPlatter: New Products, New Software, and a Network. *Laserdisk Professional* 289 (March, 1990): 17-22.

Pemberton, Jeffery K. Online interviews Marty Kahn, president, BRS. *Online* 12:1 (January, 1988): 13-19.

Perry, Edwin M. The Ezekiel Effect--Factors Affecting Development of Local Area Networks for CD-ROM. *Laserdisk Professional* 3:1 (January, 1990): 7-9.

Power, Kevin. Agencies armed with CD-ROM, LANs to stretch stingy budget. (General Services Administration Office of Technical Assistance Dir. John Caron). *Government Computer News* 9:6 (March 19, 1990): 106.

Raskin, Robin. Multimedia: the next frontier for business? (Software Review). *PC Magazine* 9:13 (July, 1990): 151ss.

Ricciardi, Salvatore P. Faster throughput tops list of Lantastic 3.0's features. (Software Review). *PC Week* 7:29 (July 23, 1990): 37-38.

Rosen, Linda. CD-Networks and CD-ROM: distributing data on disk. Online 14:4 (July, 1990): 102-105.

Rutherford, John. Improving CD-ROM Management Through Networking. *CD-ROM Professional* 3:5 (September, 1990): 20-27.

Schuyler, Chet and Lori Meads. Cheyenne Software Inc.: Monitrix 1.1. (Software Review) (one of four network management utility evaluations in 'NetWare Tools Relieves LAN Headaches'). *PC Week* 7:26 (July 2, 1990): 71-2.

Schwartz, Evan. Lotus diversifies line with CD-ROM products; seeks alternative to PC ups and downs. (product announcement). *Computer Systems News* No. 393 (November 21, 1988): 52.

Schwerin, Julie B. Optical Publishing: life in the fast lane. *Information Today* 6:6 (June 1, 1989): 22-23.

Seymour, Jim. In chasing the corporate dollar, network vendors neglect the cheap and easy solutions needed in homes and small offices. *PC Magazine* 8:18(October 31, 1989): 79-80.

Shalvoy, Mary Lee. Making inroads: peer-to-peer networking opens doors. Computer Reseller News (July 30 1990): n379, 91(1).

Sloan, Stephen. The Networked CD-ROM System: Gathering Information Through the User Interface. *CD-ROM Professional* 3:4 (July, 1990): 25-29.

St. Clair, Melanie. Event aims at meeting federal market needs. (Federal Computer Conference). *LAN Times* 7:9 (September, 1990): 37.

Stewart, Linda, K. Chiang and B. Coons. *Public Access CD-ROMs in Libraries: Case Studies*. Westport, CT: Meckler, 1990.

Stock, K. F. Cataloguing and OPAC with compact disc in a local area network and in regional bibliographic utilities. *ABI-Tech.* 9:3 (1989): 183-188.

Sullivan, Kristina B. HP's LaserROM/LAN offers network access to CD-ROM service. (product announcement). *PC Week* 6:31 (August 7, 1989): 50.

Tenopir, Carol. What's happening with CD-ROM, part 2: networks and more. *Library Journal* 114:18 (November 1, 1989): 68, 70.

Thompson, M. Keith and Kimberly Maxwell. Advanced Graphic Applications Inc. AGANET. (Hardware Review) (one of six evaluations of CD-ROM networking hardware and software in 'Networking CD-ROMs.'). *PC Magazine* 9:4 (February 27, 1990): 242-243.

---------- Artisoft Inc. LANtastic. (Software Review) (one of six evaluations of CD-ROM networking hardware and software in 'Networking CD-ROMs.'). *PC Magazine* 9:4 (February 27, 1990): 245-246.

---------- CBIS Inc. CD Server. (Hardware Review) (one of six evaluations of CD-ROM networking hardware and software in 'Networking CD-ROMs.'). *PC Magazine* 9:4 (February 27, 1990): 250-251.

---------- Fresh Technology Group Map Assist. (Software Review) (one of six evaluations of CD-ROM networking hardware and software in 'Networking CD-ROMs.') *PC Magazine* 9:4. (February 27, 1990): 252-253.

---------- Hewlett-Packard Co. HP OfficeShare. (Software Review) (one of six evaluations of CD-ROM networking hardware and software in 'Networking CD-ROMs.'). *PC Magazine* 9:4. (February 27, 1990): 256-257.

---------- Networking CD-ROMs. (Hardware Review) (overview of six evaluations of CD-ROM LAN servers)(includes related articles on CD-ROM products and the Editor's Choice). *PC Magazine* 9:4. (February 27, 1990): 237ss.

---------- Online Computer Systems Inc. Opti-Net. (Hardware Review) (one of six evaluations of CD-ROM networking hardware and software in 'Networking CD-ROMs.') *PC Magazine* 9:4 (February 27, 1990): 259-260.

Thyfault, Mary E. Distributed computing users set for CD-ROM, study says; as prices go down, CD-ROM is positioned as competitor to popular media. *MIS Week* 11:5 (January 29, 1990): 19-20.

Udell, Jon and Rob Mitchell. LANtastic. (evaluation of Artisoft Inc's low-cost peer-to-peer local area network). *Byte* 15:6 (June, 1990): 145-147.

---------- MainLAN. (evaluation of US Sage Inc's MainLAN 2.14 peer-to-peer MS-DOS local area network). *Byte* 15:6 (June, 1990): 156-157.

---------- Networks of peers: flexible, low-cost LANs do their fair share. (seven low-cost peer-to-peer local-area networks are reviewed in related articles) (buyers guide). *Byte* 15:6 (June 1990) pp.: 142, 144-6, 148, 150, 152-4, 156, 158, 160, 162.

---------- ReadyNet. (evaluation of Corvus Systems' ReadyNet 1.0 low-cost peer-to-peer local area network). *Byte* 15:6 (June, 1990): 148-149.

Van Name, Mark L. and Bill Catching. A natural match. (CBIS's CD Server/CD Connection and Online Computer Systems' Opti-Net are two solutions to the problem of adding a CD-ROM drive to a local-area network) (column). *Byte* 15:6 (June, 1990): 109-111.

---------- A natural match (CD-ROMs and LANs). *OCLC Micro* 6:3 (June 1990): 13-19, 22.

Venditto, Gus. Pipeline. (Lan manager file system borrows minicomputer (column). *PC Magazine* 8:13 (July, 1989): 63-4.

Watson, Bradley and Jon Fausey. Relative performance of three CD-ROM network access products. *OCLC Micro* 5:4 (August 1, 1989): 20-21.

---------- Relative performance of two more CD-ROM network access products. *OCLC Micro* 6:3 (June, 1990): 14-15.

Williams, Suzanne F. Networking extensions help solve problems with multiple access to data. *PC Week* 5:31 (August 1, 1988): 52.

Woods, Wendy. HP networks CD-ROMs. (product announcement). *Newsbytes* (July 11, 1989).

Zengerle, Patricia.   CD-ROM is in bloom as products debut. *MIS Week* 9:10 (March 7, 1988): 1+.

Index

About the Contributors

Ka-Neng Au joined the John Cotton Dana Library of Rutgers University as a Reference Librarian and Business Bibliographer in 1986. He became the Microcomputer Coordinator for the Rutgers-Newark libraries as well. He designed and implemented the technical aspects of three CD-ROM LANs at the Dana Library. These ranked among the first CD-ROM network installations in the country. Of the three networks, two consist of Token-Ring LANs in an IBM PC LAN environment. One consists of a type 3a and the other a type 3b network. The third one uses LANtastic hardware and software and a CD Net tower. Au appears frequently on conference programs. He has spoken on the networking of CD-ROM in both the U.S. and Europe. He is currently Vice-Chair/Chair-Elect of ALA/LITA's Optical Information Systems Group.

Joyce Demmitt joined the staff of Howard County Library in 1970 as a library associate. She worked as Branch Manager of several Howard County Library facilities, Coordinator of Reader's Advisory Services, Head of Adult Services, and, since 1986, Department Head of Information Services. She is an avid proponent of the incorporation of technology into information services. She has the primary responsibility for review and selection of databases available on Howard County Library's INFO-LAN network as well as for negotiating license agreements with vendors.

Norman Desmarais is editor-in-chief of *CD-ROM Librarian*, author of *The Librarian's CD-ROM Handbook* and *Acquisitions Systems for Libraries*, and editor of *CD-ROMs In Print*. As a beta tester for BiblioFile, he has been involved with CD-ROM since 1985. He writes and speaks frequently about CD-ROM. He teaches courses in management information systems and new and emerging computer technologies in the Graduate School of Business at Providence College in Providence, R.I. In his spare time, Norman works as acquisitions librarian at Providence College where he has set up two networks. One uses LANtastic's Network Operating System on an Ethernet configuration. The other network supports seven stations using Opti-Net CD-ROM networking software running on Novell. It incorporates four 4-drive units and two Pioneer minichangers.

Norma Hill joined the Howard County Library staff in 1980 as Nonfiction Department Head. She became Assistant Director in 1981. Prior to working for Howard County, she worked as an Information Management Specialist at the Executive Office of the President/White House Information Center after returning from Ramstein, Germany, where she managed an Air Force Library. Ms. Hill has been involved in all technological improvements at the Howard County Library and was the driving force in the development and implementation of INFO-LAN. She served as project manager and, in that capacity, developed the implementation timetable, selected the hardware, and oversaw the installation of the network. She currently heads the project team working on dial-in access to INFO-LAN.

Mark Leggott of OPTIM, a Canadian CD-ROM publisher, is responsible for the design and technical development for many of OPTIM'S products. He also provides technical support for the sale of CD-ROM hardware and software development tools. He has had extensive working experience with PCs, CD-ROM, online databases, and networks in library environments. He worked at the University of New Brunswick as Information Transfer Coordinator, which involved him in many aspects of information management and library automation technology as well as in the setting up of that library's CD-ROM network. He has also operated his own research and consulting business in Fredericton and worked as the librarian with the New Brunswick Department of Natural Resources and Energy. He is a columnist and software reviewer for several information technology magazines and has published a number of articles on CD-ROM and Local Area Networks. He is currently the national coordinator of the Canadian Library Association's largest interest group called the Canadian CD-ROM Interest Group. Mark also speaks frequently on topics of library automation, CD-ROM, and LANs in libraries.

Meta Nissley is Head of Acquisitions and Collection Management at California State University, Chico. She is a member of the advisory board of *CD-ROM Librarian* where she has had several articles published and she is coeditor of *CD-ROM Licensing and Copyright Issues for Libraries*. She has also written for *Library Acquisitions: Practice and Theory*, *Library Software Review*, *Technicalities*, and *The Acquisitions Librarian*. Her library selected the EBSCO CD-ROM Network configuration. Meta researched and negotiated the licensing agreements for the CD-ROM subscriptions at California State University, Chico.

Oliver Pesch is the Director of Technical Development for EBSCO Electronic Information, a division of EBSCO Industries which is involved in the development and marketing of CD-ROM products. Besides directing the development of the search and retrieval software for EBSCO's CD-ROM products, Oliver is also responsible for the introduction of the EBSCO CD-ROM Network which uses the LANtastic Network Operating System and Opti-Net CD-ROM networking software running on either LANtastic's own proprietary network hardware or on Ethernet hardware. Prior to joining EBSCO in 1986, he was Manager of Development and Support for Sydney Development Corporation's Library Automation Products division. He has been involved in the development of software for the automation of libraries since 1981.

George A. Sands, Jr. is Library Administrator of the Caroline County Public Library in Maryland. He organized the library as the county's information center and developed a unique local area network featuring office automation and network use of CD-ROM databases, including branch library remote access. He is currenty working on development of countywide remote access to the network. He has spearheaded a regionwide CD-ROM union database project. George has spoken about CD-ROM networking at many conferences; and he participated in the CD-ROM II teleconference at the College of Dupage, Illinios in 1989.